THE CIVIL WAR
QUIZ BOOK

OSPREY
PUBLISHING

THE CIVIL WAR
QUIZ BOOK

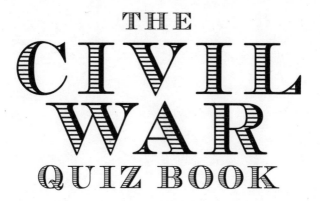

First published in Great Britain in 2012 by Osprey Publishing,
Midland House, West Way, Botley, Oxford, OX2 0PH, UK
44-02 23rd Street, Suite 219, Long Island City, NY 11101, USA

E-mail: info@ospreypublishing.com

Osprey Publishing is part of the Osprey Group

A CIP catalog record for this book is available from the British Library.

Joseph McCullough has asserted his right under the Copyright, Designs and Patents Act,
1988, to be identified as the Author of this Work.

Print ISBN: 978 1 84908 618 9
PDF eBook ISBN: 978 1 78096 395 2
ePub ISBN: 978 1 78096 396 9

Page layout by Myriam Bell Designs, UK
Typeset in Bembo, AT Chevalier, Bernard MT Condensed and 1Stone Serif
Cover originated by PDQ Media, Bungay, UK
Printed in China through Worldprint Ltd.

12 13 14 15 16   10 9 8 7 6 5 4 3 2 1

Osprey Publishing is supporting the Woodland Trust, the UK's leading woodland conservation
charity, by funding the dedication of trees.

Front cover image courtesy Library of Congress. All images not otherwise credited are
courtesy Library of Congress.

The author would like to thank Rufus Thurston for the Anagrams.

www.ospreypublishing.com

EASY QUESTIONS

ONE-STAR GENERAL KNOWLEDGE

QUIZ 1
MULTIPLE CHOICE

1. What was the first state to secede from the Union?

   ❏ a. Mississippi ❏ b. North Carolina
   ❏ c. South Carolina ❏ d. Georgia

2. Who was Robert E. Lee's "Old Warhorse"?

   ❏ a. James Longstreet
   ❏ b. Thomas J. "Stonewall" Jackson
   ❏ c. J.E.B. Stuart
   ❏ d. A.P. Hill

3. Who commanded the Union Army during the 1862 battle of Antietam?

   ❏ a. George Meade ❏ b. Joseph Hooker
   ❏ c. George B. McClellan ❏ d. Ulysses S. Grant

4. In which year was the "Battle of the Crater" fought?

   ❏ a. 1861 ❏ b. 1862
   ❏ c. 1863 ❏ d. 1864

DID YOU KNOW...

Confederate general Joseph Wheeler, who was less than 30 years old when the war ended, was later called into the service of the US Army during the Spanish-American War. In 1898, Wheeler fought in Cuba alongside a number of young US officers, including John J. Pershing.

5. Which of the following is often labelled the first land battle of the war?

☐ a. Pea Ridge   ☐ b. Big Bethel
☐ c. Ball's Bluff   ☐ d. First Bull Run

6. What fruit was Thomas J. "Stonewall" Jackson famous for consuming while on campaign?

☐ a. oranges   ☐ b. lemons
☐ c. bananas   ☐ d. apples

7. From which state do "tarheels" originate?

☐ a. Alabama   ☐ b. Kentucky
☐ c. South Carolina   ☐ d. North Carolina

8. Which of these was a color commonly worn by Confederate troops?

☐ a. osage   ☐ b. butternut
☐ c. okra   ☐ d. Tennessee green

9. The "Hornet's Nest" was a feature of which battle?

☐ a. Shiloh   ☐ b. Gettysburg
☐ c. Chickamauga   ☐ d. Chancellorsville

10. Who was "Old Blue Light"?

☐ a. Robert E. Lee
☐ b. Albert Sidney Johnston
☐ c. Thomas J. "Stonewall" Jackson
☐ d. J.E.B. Stuart

QUIZ 2
TRUE OR FALSE

1. Early in the war, William T. Sherman was given a "mental leave of absence" after apparently suffering a mental breakdown.
   ❑ True   ❑ False

2. Abraham Lincoln offered Robert E. Lee command of the entire US Army.
   ❑ True   ❑ False

3. Robert E. Lee gave up smoking during the war.
   ❑ True   ❑ False

© Simon Tofield

4. Nathan Bedford Forrest had no military training prior to the Civil War.
   ❑ True ❑ False

5. More combined casualties were suffered during Antietam than in any battle except Gettysburg.
   ❑ True ❑ False

6. During the battle of the Wilderness, James Longstreet was mistakenly shot by Confederate troops.
   ❑ True ❑ False

7. Union troops provided transportation to citizens wishing to leave Atlanta before it was burned.
   ❑ True ❑ False

8. During the battle of Fredericksburg, "Stonewall" Jackson held the left half of the Confederate line.
   ❑ True ❑ False

9. Confederate general Richard Taylor was the grandson of former US President Zachary Taylor.
   ❑ True ❑ False

10. The Citadel Military Institute in Charleston was established during the war.
    ❑ True ❑ False

I wish he was in Congress or a Bar Room, anywhere but our army.

William T. Sherman on General Francis Preston Blair

QUIZ 3
SHORT ANSWER

1. Whom did Abraham Lincoln call "Father Neptune"?

   . . . .

2. Which battle was fought first, Chickamauga or Chattanooga?

   . . . .

3. What is the more famous name of the "Black Hat Brigade"?

   . . . .

4. Which battlefield contained the two "Round Tops"?

   . . . .

5. Who was President of the United States when South Carolina seceded?

   . . . .

THE VOLUNTARY MANNER IN WHICH SOME OF THE SOUTHERN VOLUNTEERS ENLIST.

6. What was the "Peculiar Institution"?

. . . .

7. In theory, an infantry regiment contained how many men?

. . . .

8. Which side first sent an army into neutral Kentucky, the Union or the Confederacy?

. . . .

9. Which fort was captured by the Union first, Fort Henry or Fort Donelson?

. . . .

10. Who became President first, Abraham Lincoln or Jefferson Davis?

. . . .

> *You may appear much concerned at my attacking on Sunday.*
> *I am greatly concerned, too: but I felt it my duty to do it.*
>
> Thomas J. "Stonewall" Jackson

QUIZ 4
MULTIPLE CHOICE

1. Prior to the battle of Antietam, a Union soldier discovered a copy of Lee's battle plan being used as a wrapper for what?

   ❏ a. bread   ❏ b. coffee
   ❏ c. a photograph   ❏ d. cigars

2. What was the first battle in which Ulysses S. Grant faced Robert E. Lee?

   ❏ a. Cold Harbor   ❏ b. Spotsylvania Courthouse
   ❏ c. the Wilderness   ❏ d. Fredericksburg

3. Drewry's Bluff served as part of the defense of which city?

   ❏ a. Richmond   ❏ b. Charleston
   ❏ c. Washington, D.C.   ❏ d. Atlanta

4. Which of these battles was NOT fought in Tennessee?

   ❏ a. Chickamauga   ❏ b. Chattanooga
   ❏ c. Stone's River   ❏ d. Fort Donelson

5. Who became President upon the death of Abraham Lincoln?

   ❏ a. John Tyler   ❏ b. James Buchanan
   ❏ c. Franklin Pierce   ❏ d. Andrew Johnson

6. What was the most populous city in the Union at the outbreak of the war?

   ❏ a. New York   ❏ b. Chicago
   ❏ c. Washington, D.C.   ❏ d. Buffalo

7. What was the largest "all-cavalry" battle of the war?

   ❑ a. Sabine Crossroads ❑ b. Yellow Tavern
   ❑ c. Brandy Station ❑ d. Yellow Ford

8. Marye's Heights was a feature of which battlefield?

   ❑ a. Chancellorsville ❑ b. Gettysburg
   ❑ c. Chattanooga ❑ d. Fredericksburg

9. What is a "kepi"?

   ❑ a. saddle ❑ b. raincoat
   ❑ c. hat ❑ d. tent

10. During the war, how many stars flew on the flag of Texas?

   ❑ a. 0 ❑ b. 1
   ❑ c. 2 ❑ d. 3

DID YOU KNOW...

When John Fremont learned that Lincoln intended to remove him from command of the Department of the West, he ordered his pickets to refuse admittance to any soldier coming from Washington. Thus, the captain tasked with delivering the relief order disguised himself as a farmer and claimed to have information on Confederate movements. Thus gaining admittance, he delivered the orders and was immediately placed under arrest. The captain soon escaped, and Fremont relinquished his command.

MATCH UP

Match these battles with another name for the same battle.

1. Antietam   a) Seven Pines

2. Fair Oaks   b) Stone's River

3. Cedar Creek   c) Pea Ridge

4. First Manassas   d) Chaplin Hills

5. Perryville   e) Pittsburg Landing

6. Murfreesboro   f) Sharpsburg

7. Wilson's Creek   g) Opequon Creek

8. Shiloh   h) Oak Hills

9. Winchester   i) Belle Grove

10. Elkhorn Tavern   j) Bull Run

QUIZ 6
MULTIPLE CHOICE

1. Which ship finally sank the famed CSS *Alabama*?

   ❏ a. USS *Hatteras*   ❏ b. USS *Kearsarge*
   ❏ c. USS *Cairo*   ❏ d. USS *Wachusett*

2. On which Civil War battlefield can you still see "Bloody Lane"?

   ❏ a. Antietam   ❏ b. Gettysburg
   ❏ c. Fredericksburg   ❏ d. Chancellorsville

3. The .44 Colt Repeating Rifle held how many rounds in its cylinder?

   ❏ a. 4   ❏ b. 6
   ❏ c. 8   ❏ d. 10

4. Which Confederate general was brother-in-law to Thomas J. "Stonewall" Jackson?

   ❏ a. A.P. Hill   ❏ b. D.H. Hill
   ❏ c. J.E.B. Stuart   ❏ d. James Longstreet

> *The day you make soldiers of Negroes is the beginning of the end of the revolution. If slaves will make good soldiers our whole theory of slavery is wrong.*
>
> Howell Cobb

5. The 1861 battle of Ball's Bluff was fought adjacent to which river?

   ❏ a. James
   ❏ b. Rappahannock
   ❏ c. Potomac
   ❏ d. Catawba

6. Who led the bloody Confederate raid against Independence, Missouri?

   ❏ a. William T. Anderson
   ❏ b. Champ Ferguson
   ❏ c. John S. Mosby
   ❏ d. William C. Quantrill

7. What color uniform did the United States Sharpshooters wear?

   ❏ a. blue
   ❏ b. green
   ❏ c. brown
   ❏ d. blue and red

8. Which battle included the "Devil's Den"?

   ❏ a. Gettysburg
   ❏ b. Chickamauga
   ❏ c. Shiloh
   ❏ d. Antietam

9. In which state were the Palmetto Guards formed?

   ❏ a. Virginia
   ❏ b. North Carolina
   ❏ c. South Carolina
   ❏ d. Alabama

10. Which of these battlefields is farthest north?

    ❏ a. Antietam
    ❏ b. Gettysburg
    ❏ c. Manassas
    ❏ d. Nashville

DID YOU KNOW...

Kennesaw Mountain is named after the Cherokee word for "burial ground."

QUIZ 7
TRUE OR FALSE

EASY

1. "Stonewall" Jackson was a citizen of both the United States and the United Kingdom.
   ❑ True   ❑ False

2. Robert E. Lee graduated first in his class at West Point.
   ❑ True   ❑ False

3. The Union had a general named Jefferson Davis.
   ❑ True   ❑ False

4. Ulysses S. Grant was the first man in American history to bear the rank of lieutenant-general.
   ❑ True   ❑ False

5. Just below 50 percent of battlefield amputees survived.
   ❑ True   ❑ False

6. Abraham Lincoln was the first American president to be assassinated.
   ❑ True   ❑ False

7. Confederate general John Hunt Morgan was known during his lifetime as "The Wizard of the Saddle."
   ❑ True   ❑ False

8. More men died in prisoner-of-war camps during the war than from wounds sustained on the battlefield.
   ❑ True   ❑ False

9. During the Civil War, all telegraph messages were sent in Morse code.
   ❑ True   ❑ False

10. Confederate forces in Vicksburg surrendered "unconditionally."
    ❑ True   ❑ False

QUIZ 8
SHORT ANSWER

1. What was the commonly used nickname for the Confederate guerrilla leader William T. Anderson?

. . . .

2. In what state was Andersonville Prison?

. . . .

3. Who formed the 1st Regiment of United States Sharpshooters?

. . . .

4. What was described as a "tin can on a shingle"?

. . . .

5. Which state seceded first, Alabama or Georgia?

. . . .

6. Which Union general was "older than the Constitution"?

. . . .

7. Who was Secretary of War of the United States under Abraham Lincoln?

. . . .

8. Who was the first Grand Wizard of the Ku Klux Klan?

. . . .

9. What was George B. McClellan's middle name?

. . . .

10. Which was bigger, a regiment or a battalion?

. . . .

QUIZ 9
MULTIPLE CHOICE, ABRAHAM LINCOLN

1. How old was Abraham Lincoln when he became President of the United States?

    ❑ a. 45   ❑ b. 47
    ❑ c. 49   ❑ d. 52

2. How many men had held the position of President of the United States before Lincoln?

    ❑ a. 12   ❑ b. 14
    ❑ c. 15   ❑ d. 16

3. In what state was Lincoln born?

    ❑ a. Illinois   ❑ b. Indiana
    ❑ c. Kentucky   ❑ d. Kansas

4. In 1858, Lincoln participated in a series of seven debates with which other famous American statesman?

    ❑ a. Stephen Douglas   ❑ b. John C. Calhoun
    ❑ c. Henry Clay   ❑ d. Jefferson Davis

5. Who was Lincoln's first Vice-President?

    ❑ a. Andrew Johnson   ❑ b. John C. Breckinridge
    ❑ c. Edwin M. Stanton   ❑ d. Hannibal Hamlin

6. Which of these states did Lincoln NOT win in the 1860 presidential election?

    ❑ a. New York   ❑ b. California
    ❑ c. Maine   ❑ d. Maryland

7. Lincoln's earliest memories were of which farm, where he lived from when he was two to when he was seven?

- ❑ a. Silver Springs Farm
- ❑ b. Knob Creek Farm
- ❑ c. Cedarhurst Farm
- ❑ d. Twin Pines Farm

8. Who was Lincoln's first child?

- ❑ a. Robert Todd Lincoln
- ❑ b. William Wallace Lincoln
- ❑ c. Edward Baker Lincoln
- ❑ d. Thomas Lincoln

9. Lincoln served as a militia captain during which war?

- ❑ a. Mexican–American War
- ❑ b. Seminole War
- ❑ c. Black Hawk War
- ❑ d. Utah War

10. Which of these states did Lincoln NOT win in the 1864 election?

- ❑ a. Illinois
- ❑ b. New York
- ❑ c. Pennsylvania
- ❑ d. New Jersey

LINCOLN'S LAST WARNING.

"Now, if you don't come down, I'll cut the Tree *from under you*."

QUIZ 10
MATCH UP

Match these Civil War leaders with the battles in which they were killed or mortally wounded.

1. Thomas J. "Stonewall" Jackson   a) Petersburg

2. Albert Sidney Johnston   b) Spotsylvania Courthouse

3. J.E.B. Stuart   c) Shiloh

4. John F. Reynolds   d) South Mountain

5. Barnard E. Bee   e) Gettysburg

6. Ben McCulloch   f) Yellow Tavern

7. States Rights Gist   g) Pea Ridge

8. John Sedgwick   h) Chancellorsville

9. A.P. Hill   i) Franklin

10. Jesse L. Reno   j) First Bull Run

QUIZ 11
MULTIPLE CHOICE

1. Which battle included bloody fighting on "Missionary Ridge"?

   ❑ a. Stone's River   ❑ b. Perryville
   ❑ c. Chickamauga   ❑ d. Chattanooga

2. How many rounds were held in the typical cartridge box carried by the soldiers of both sides during the war?

   ❑ a. 20   ❑ b. 30
   ❑ c. 40   ❑ d. 50

3. Which of these was NOT a feature of the battle of Gettysburg?

   ❑ a. the Wheat Field   ❑ b. the Peach Orchard
   ❑ c. the Sunken Road   ❑ d. the Devil's Den

4. In what year was the battle of Second Bull Run fought?

   ❑ a. 1861   ❑ b. 1862
   ❑ c. 1863   ❑ d. 1864

5. In which battle did John Bell Hood receive the wound that cost him his leg?

   ❑ a. Antietam   ❑ b. Gettysburg
   ❑ c. Chickamauga   ❑ d. the Wilderness

6. Before the secession of South Carolina in 1861, the Union contained how many states?

    ❑ a. 29   ❑ b. 31

    ❑ c. 32   ❑ d. 34

7. Which modern state contains most of the Civil War's "Indian Territory"?

    ❑ a. Arizona   ❑ b. Utah

    ❑ c. Oklahoma   ❑ d. Colorado

8. Which of these battles was NOT one of the "Seven Days Battles"?

    ❑ a. Sayler's Creek   ❑ b. Mechanicsville

    ❑ c. White Oak Swamp ❑ d. Oak Grove

9. Who founded the American Red Cross?

    ❑ a. Mary Edwards Walker ❑ b. Sarah Emma Evans

    ❑ c. Clara Barton   ❑ d. Susan Baker

10. Which city was Fort Negley built to defend?

    ❑ a. Nashville   ❑ b. Jackson

    ❑ c. Richmond   ❑ d. Atlanta

ANAGRAMS

"Hairball Conman"

(Answers on page 216)

QUIZ 12
TRUE OR FALSE

1. There are no Confederate veterans buried in Arlington National Cemetery.
   ❑ True   ❑ False

2. There are fewer than 20 known unique photographs of Abraham Lincoln.
   ❑ True   ❑ False

3. Robert E. Lee was the son of Revolutionary War general Charles Lee.
   ❑ True   ❑ False

4. North Carolina was the last state to officially join the Confederacy.
   ❑ True   ❑ False

5. Thomas J. "Stonewall" Jackson was orphaned as a child.
   ❑ True   ❑ False

DID YOU KNOW...

During his days in the regular army, Braxton Bragg once served as both commander and quartermaster to a company at a remote outpost. At one point, acting as a company commander, he submitted a requisition for supplies, but turned it down in his role as quartermaster. He then resubmitted the requisition with further reasons why the supplies were necessary, but once again, his quartermaster half refused.

6. Ulysses S. Grant served two terms as President of the United States.
   ❏ True   ❏ False

7. Taking into account Union and Confederate soldiers, more Americans died in the Civil War than in any other conflict.
   ❏ True   ❏ False

8. General Joseph Hooker never graduated from West Point.
   ❏ True   ❏ False

9. Union general Abner Doubleday invented baseball as a way for his men to pass the time in camp.
   ❏ True   ❏ False

10. "The last grand charge of the Army of Tennessee" occurred in North Carolina.
    ❏ True   ❏ False

QUIZ 13
SHORT ANSWER

1. After West Virginia was made a state, how many stars did Old Glory contain?

. . . .

2. Who was the first head of the Union Intelligence Service?

. . . .

RICHMOND NEWSBOY ANNOUNCING THE REBEL SUCCESS!!!

3. On a LeMat revolver, which barrel fired the shot-charge, the top or the bottom?

. . . .

4. How do you make a "Quaker Gun"?

. . . .

5. Who was the first Confederate Secretary of the Navy?

. . . .

6. Who wrote *Uncle Tom's Cabin*?

. . . .

7. What city was known as "The turntable of the Confederacy"?

. . . .

8. Which Confederate general was also the Episcopal bishop of Louisiana?

. . . .

9. Who was the British Prime Minister at the outbreak of the Civil War?

. . . .

10. Who was the last commander of the Army of the Potomac?

. . . .

> *Vicksburg is the key. The war can never be brought to a close until that key is in our pocket.*
>
> Abraham Lincoln

QUIZ 14
MULTIPLE CHOICE

1. Which Union general has a bridge named after him on the Antietam battlefield?

   ❏ a. John Sedgwick ❏ b. John Porter Hatch
   ❏ c. Ambrose Burnside ❏ d. George Sykes

2. Who commanded the Army of the Potomac at First Manassas?

   ❏ a. Irvin McDowell ❏ b. Joseph E. Johnston
   ❏ c. P.G.T. Beauregard ❏ d. Robert Patterson

3. The first official flag of the Confederate States of America contained how many stripes?

   ❏ a. 0 ❏ b. 3
   ❏ c. 4 ❏ d. 6

4. Which of these battles was NOT fought in North Carolina?

   ❏ a. Bentonville ❏ b. Roanoke Island
   ❏ c. Wyse Fork ❏ d. Honey Hill

5. Apart from West Virginia, what was the only other territory to achieve statehood during the war?

   ❏ a. California ❏ b. Utah
   ❏ c. Nevada ❏ d. Colorado

6. On April 15, just after the surrender of Fort Sumter, Lincoln called for how many volunteers to put down the rebellion?

   ❑ a. 30,000   ❑ b. 75,000
   ❑ c. 100,000   ❑ d. 150,000

7. "Morgan's Christmas Raid" included Christmas of which year?

   ❑ a. 1861   ❑ b. 1862
   ❑ c. 1863   ❑ d. 1864

8. Which Union cavalry officer was famous for his love of dogs?

   ❑ a. Philip Sheridan   ❑ b. George A. Custer
   ❑ c. Benjamin Grierson   ❑ d. John Buford

9. Which one of these Civil War commanders was NOT bald?

   ❑ a. D.H. Hill   ❑ b. Ambrose Burnside
   ❑ c. Richard Ewell   ❑ d. Benjamin Butler

10. How many masts did the CSS *Alabama* have?

   ❑ a. 0   ❑ b. 2
   ❑ c. 3   ❑ d. 4

> *I think it better to do right, even if we suffer in so doing, than to incur the reproach of our consciences and posterity.*
>
> Robert E. Lee declining to hang prisoners in retaliation for Union destruction.

QUIZ 15
MATCH UP

Match these Civil War leaders with their nicknames.

1. Henry Halleck   a) Old Bald Head

2. John S. Mosby   b) The Grey Ghost

3. Thomas J. Jackson   c) Lo

4. Edward Johnson   d) Old Brains

5. John A. Logan   e) Stonewall

6. Nathan Evans   f) Allegheny

7. William T. Sherman   g) Old Blizzards

8. Richard S. Ewell   h) Cump

9. William L. Loring   i) Shanks

10. Lewis Armistead   j) Black Jack

QUIZ 16
MULTIPLE CHOICE

1. Who led the Army of the Potomac on its infamous "Mud March" in 1863?

   □ a. George Meade   □ b. Joseph Hooker
   □ c. Ambrose Burnside   □ d. Ulysses S. Grant

2. Which general took command of the Confederate forces at Shiloh after the fall of Albert Sidney Johnston?

   □ a. Braxton Bragg   □ b. William Hardee
   □ c. John Bell Hood   □ d. P.G.T. Beauregard

3. Which of these battles occurred last chronologically?

   □ a. Savage Station   □ b. Fair Oaks
   □ c. Mechanicsville   □ d. Gaines's Mill

4. Which battle included the "Hornets' Nest"?

   □ a. Chickamauga   □ b. Chattanooga
   □ c. Shiloh   □ d. Vicksburg

5. Who led the Confederate forces at the 1864 battle of New Market?

   □ a. Jubal Early   □ b. John C. Breckinridge
   □ c. Kirby Smith   □ d. John Bell Hood

6. Who wrote *A Diary from Dixie*?

   □ a. Clara Barton   □ b. Mary Chestnut
   □ c. Georgiana Walker   □ d. Harriet Beecher Stowe

7. What color legs did notorious Kansas Jayhawkers supposedly possess?

☐ a. black   ☐ b. blue
☐ c. red   ☐ d. yellow

8. During the Civil War, what was the maximum number of companies a cavalry regiment could contain?

☐ a. 4   ☐ b. 6
☐ c. 8   ☐ d. 12

9. In which battle was Ben McCulloch killed?

☐ a. Perryville   ☐ b. Pea Ridge
☐ c. Murfreesboro ☐ d. Shiloh

10. Which Union commander went on to lead the United States force against the Nez Perce Indians in 1877?

☐ a. George A. Custer ☐ b. Philip Sheridan
☐ c. Oliver Howard   ☐ d. George Stoneman

DID YOU KNOW...

During the battle of Mine Creek, Union private James Dunlavy singlehandedly captured the Confederate cavalry general John Marmaduke. Taking his prisoner to his department headquarters, Dunlavy immediately received an eight-month furlough, the full amount of his remaining period of enlistment.

QUIZ 17
TRUE OR FALSE

1. Joshua Chamberlain was never wounded during the war.
   ❑ True   ❑ False

2. J.E.B. Stuart was a teetotaler.
   ❑ True   ❑ False

3. The Gatling gun was never deployed during the war.
   ❑ True   ❑ False

4. George B. McClellan was sent as an observer to the Crimean War.
   ❑ True   ❑ False

5. Winfield Scott had served as commander of the US Army for nearly 20 years before the outbreak of the Civil War.
   ❑ True   ❑ False

6. George Washington Custis Lee was the eldest son of Robert E. Lee.
   ❑ True   ❑ False

7. After the battle of Chancellorsville, General Joseph Hooker never commanded troops in battle again.
   ❑ True   ❑ False

8. Although indicted for treason, Jefferson Davis was never sent to prison.
   ❑ True   ❑ False

9. During the Civil War, the term "Legion" denoted a regiment with over 1,000 men.
   ❑ True   ❑ False

10. Nathan Bedford Forrest was a millionaire before the war.
    ❑ True   ❑ False

SHORT ANSWER

1. Who was the first colonel of the 54th Massachusetts Volunteer Infantry?

   . . . .

2. Which Union general was sometimes called "Forty-eight Hours"?

   . . . .

3. Discounting West Virginia, how many slave-holding "border states" did NOT secede from the Union?

   . . . .

4. What was the first capital of the Confederacy?

   . . . .

SOUTHERN ASS-STOCK-CRAZY.
(SOUTHERN ARISTOCRACY.)

5. Which Union general smoked a cigar to prove he was alive as he was carried away from the Gettysburg battlefield?

....

6. Did the Army of the Kanawha belong to the Union or the Confederacy?

....

7. In what state was the Confederate Naval School?

....

8. Who did Robert E. Lee call "my bad old man"?

....

9. What firearm was issued to the United States Sharpshooter regiments?

....

10. On average, which side's divisions contained more brigades, the North or South?

....

> *So great is my confidence in General Lee that I am willing to follow him blindfolded.*
>
> Thomas J. "Stonewall" Jackson

MULTIPLE CHOICE, THE VICKSBURG CAMPAIGN

1. Who surrendered Vicksburg to General Ulysses S. Grant?

   - a. Joseph E. Johnston
   - b. John C. Pemberton
   - c. Earl Van Dorn
   - d. Richard Taylor

2. Who led the Union assault against Chickasaw Bluffs?

   - a. John A. Rawlings
   - b. John A. McClernand
   - c. James B. McPherson
   - d. William T. Sherman

3. From whose bayou did Sherman's infantry have to rescue Admiral Porter and his fleet?

   - a. Red's
   - b. Vick's
   - c. Pemberton's
   - d. Steele's

4. What was the last Confederate stronghold on the Mississippi?

   - a. Vicksburg
   - b. Fort Hindman
   - c. Fort Donelson
   - d. Port Hudson

5. Which of these actions occurred last chronologically?

   - a. Big Black River
   - b. Chickasaw Bluffs
   - c. Champion Hill
   - d. the fall of Fort Hindman

6. Which Union general led the attack that captured Fort Hindman?

   - a. John A. Rawlings
   - b. John A. McClernand
   - c. James B. McPherson
   - d. William T. Sherman

7. What was Admiral Porter's flagship during the run past Vicksburg?

   ❑ a. USS *Benton*   ❑ b. USS *Henry Clay*
   ❑ c. USS *Magnolia*   ❑ d. USS *Tuscumbia*

8. Approximately how many Confederate soldiers surrendered at Vicksburg?

   ❑ a. 22,000   ❑ b. 27,000
   ❑ c. 31,000   ❑ d. 38,000

9. Which of these was NOT a Division Leader in Pemberton's Vicksburg Army?

   ❑ a. Carter Stevenson   ❑ b. Seth Barton
   ❑ c. John Forney   ❑ d. John Bowen

10. How many days did the "Siege of Vicksburg" last?

   ❑ a. 33   ❑ b. 47
   ❑ c. 59   ❑ d. 82

> *So short lived has been the American Union that men who saw its rise may live to see its fall.*
>
> *The Times* of London

MATCH UP

Match these Civil War generals with their horses.

1. William T. Sherman   a) Virginia

2. Robert E. Lee   b) Dolly

3. J.E.B. Stuart   c) Baldy

4. Ulysses S. Grant   d) Little Sorrell

5. Philip Sheridan   e) Cincinnati

6. George Meade   f) Hero

7. George B. McClellan   g) Lookout

8. Thomas J. "Stonewall" Jackson h) Daniel Webster

9. Joseph Hooker   i) Traveller

10. James Longstreet   j) Winchester

MULTIPLE CHOICE

1. In which beleaguered city did the "Cracker Line" end?
   - ❏ a. Vicksburg
   - ❏ b. Chattanooga
   - ❏ c. Atlanta
   - ❏ d. Richmond

2. Who led the Union forces during the Red River expedition?
   - ❏ a. Hugh Kilpatrick
   - ❏ b. Peter Osterhaus
   - ❏ c. Henry Slocum
   - ❏ d. Nathaniel P. Banks

3. Which Confederate general possessed a red "battle shirt"?
   - ❏ a. D.H. Hill
   - ❏ b. A.P. Hill
   - ❏ c. James Longstreet
   - ❏ d. J.E.B. Stuart

4. From the town of Gettysburg, in which general direction is Little Round Top?
   - ❏ a. north
   - ❏ b. south
   - ❏ c. east
   - ❏ d. west

5. Jefferson Davis married the daughter of which President of the United States?
   - ❏ a. James Polk
   - ❏ b. Zachary Taylor
   - ❏ c. John Tyler
   - ❏ d. Andrew Jackson

6. The Tredegar Ironworks was located in which city?
   - ❏ a. Richmond
   - ❏ b. Atlanta
   - ❏ c. Columbia
   - ❏ d. Raleigh

7. Who led the Confederate forces during the Cheat Mountain campaign?

☐ a. Robert E. Lee
☐ b. Joseph E. Johnston
☐ c. Thomas J. "Stonewall" Jackson
☐ d. P.G.T. Beauregard

8. After the war, Robert E. Lee accepted the presidency of which school?

☐ a. University of Virginia
☐ b. Washington College
☐ c. University of the South
☐ d. College of William & Mary

9. Which of these Confederate generals was born in Washington, D.C.?

☐ a. D.H. Hill
☐ b. Richard Ewell
☐ c. A.P. Hill
☐ d. Henry Heth

10. Approximately how many men served in the United States Army in 1860?

☐ a. 4,000
☐ b. 8,000
☐ c. 12,000
☐ d. 16,000

DID YOU KNOW...

The men and woman accused of conspiring to assassinate Abraham Lincoln were kept in cells with hoods over their heads and pads over their eyes and ears. When they were brought to trial, they sat in the courtroom in shackles.

QUIZ 22
TRUE OR FALSE

1. The USS *Monitor* sank with all hands in 1862 near Cape Hatteras, North Carolina.
   ❑ True ❑ False

2. Both the Union and the Confederacy used breechloading artillery during the war.
   ❑ True ❑ False

3. Thomas J. "Stonewall" Jackson's amputated arm has its own marked grave.
   ❑ True ❑ False

4. Admiral David Farragut was a veteran of the War of 1812.
   ❑ True ❑ False

5. General John Reynolds was captured three times during the war.
   ❑ True ❑ False

6. After Antietam, the second-bloodiest day of the war occurred during the battle of Chancellorsville.
   ❑ True ❑ False

7. Only one battle between Union and Confederate forces took place in California during the war.
   ❑ True ❑ False

8. General James Longstreet was a noted poker player.
   ❑ True ❑ False

9. Confederate Joseph Orville "Jo" Shelby never surrendered.
   ❑ True ❑ False

10. Abraham Lincoln did not attend the 1864 Republican Convention.
    ❑ True ❑ False

SHORT ANSWER

1. Which Union general was famous (or infamous) for supposedly stealing spoons?

   . . . .

2. To whom did Ulysses S. Grant assign the honor of receiving the official surrender of the Army of Northern Virginia?

   . . . .

3. Which battle contained the first recorded instance of the "rebel yell"?

   . . . .

4. Who claimed victory in the "Buckland Races," the Union or the Confederacy?

   . . . .

5. Who commanded the Union Army of Virginia?

   . . . .

THE UNION   versus   SECESSION.
The Union Builds Bridges.   and   Secession Destroys Them.

6. During which battle did Robert E. Lee order a night attack for the first time?

....

7. What was the first ship to be sunk by the CSS *Virginia*?

....

8. The first "zouave" units were formed in which country?

....

9. During battle, what assignment was generally given to military bandsmen?

....

10. Which ship won the 1863 duel between the CSS *Atlanta* and the USS *Weehawken*?

....

ANAGRAMS

"Menthol Parsley"

(Answers on page 216)

QUIZ 24
MULTIPLE CHOICE

1. How many years did Robert E. Lee spend in the US Army before resigning his commission?

   ❑ a. 18   ❑ b. 26
   ❑ c. 32   ❑ d. 42

2. Which Union corps was mainly formed of colored troops?

   ❑ a. XVI   ❑ b. XIX
   ❑ c. XXII   ❑ d. XXV

3. The battle of Sailor's Creek was fought in which year?

   ❑ a. 1862   ❑ b. 1863
   ❑ c. 1864   ❑ d. 1865

4. According to US Army regulations, a volunteer infantry company was divided into how many platoons?

   ❑ a. 2   ❑ b. 3
   ❑ c. 4   ❑ d. 5

5. The Union contained how many slave-holding states before the outbreak of the war?

   ❑ a. 11   ❑ b. 13
   ❑ c. 15   ❑ d. 17

6. Before the firing on Fort Sumter, cadets from the South Carolina Military Academy stationed on Morris Island opened fire on which Federal supply ship trying reach the fort?

   ❑ a. *St. Philip*   ❑ b. *Star of the West*
   ❑ c. *Brooklyn*   ❑ d. *Havana Sally*

7. Which year saw the last Federal Census before the war?

   ❑ a. 1857   ❑ b. 1858
   ❑ c. 1859   ❑ d. 1860

8. How many stars flew on the "Bonnie Blue Flag"?

   ❑ a. 0   ❑ b. 1
   ❑ c. 2   ❑ d. 4

9. What color was used to identify troops that had never been in battle?

   ❑ a. red   ❑ b. blue
   ❑ c. yellow   ❑ d. green

10. Which of these battles in the Peninsula Campaign occurred last chronologically?

   ❑ a. Dam No. 1   ❑ b. Etham's Landing
   ❑ c. Williamsburg   ❑ d. Lee's Mill

Before this war is over, I intend to be a major-general or a corpse.

Isaac Trimble

MATCH UP

Match up these commanders with their battlefield victories.

1. First Bull Run   a) Robert E. Lee

2. McDowell   b) George B. McClellan

3. Fort Donelson   c) Ulysses S. Grant

4. Antietam   d) Ambrose Burnside

5. Chancellorsville   e) Philip Sheridan

6. Brice's Crossroads   f) P.G.T. Beauregard

7. New Bern   g) Nathan Bedford Forrest

8. Franklin   h) Joseph E. Johnston

9. Kennesaw Mountain   i) John M. Schofield

10. Cedar Creek   j) Thomas J. "Stonewall" Jackson

QUIZ 26
MULTIPLE CHOICE

1. The 1863 battle of Bristoe Station was fought in which state?

   ❑ a. Virginia   ❑ b. West Virginia
   ❑ c. Tennessee   ❑ d. Missouri

2. Who was the "Angel of the Battlefield"?

   ❑ a. Mary Edwards Walker   ❑ b. Clara Barton
   ❑ c. Dorthea Dix   ❑ d. Ruth Henry

3. Which of the following generals was NOT a brigade commander in Pickett's Division during its famous charge at Gettysburg?

   ❑ a. Lewis A. Armistead   ❑ b. J. Johnston Pettigrew
   ❑ c. Richard B. Garnett   ❑ d. James L. Kemper

4. What was Jefferson Davis' nickname at West Point?

   ❑ a. the firebrand   ❑ b. the horse trader
   ❑ c. the marble monument   ❑ d. the golden goose

5. Which Confederate general nicknamed his division "the Light Division"?

   ❑ a. D.H. Hill   ❑ b. A.P. Hill
   ❑ c. George Pickett   ❑ d. John B. Magruder

6. On what date was the battle of Franklin fought?

   ❑ a. March 18, 1864   ❑ b. July 23, 1864
   ❑ c. November 30, 1864   ❑ d. December 23, 1864

7. In what state was the battle of Sabine Crossroads fought?

   ☐ a. Louisiana   ☐ b. Mississippi
   ☐ c. Missouri   ☐ d. Texas

8. In what state would you currently find Alleghany Mountain, scene of the 1861 battle?

   ☐ a. Virginia   ☐ b. West Virginia
   ☐ c. Maryland   ☐ d. Tennessee

9. Which of these battles was NOT part of the "Overland Campaign"?

   ☐ a. Chancellorsville   ☐ b. the Wilderness
   ☐ c. Cold Harbor   ☐ d. Spotsylvania Courthouse

10. "Deep Bottom" is an area adjacent to which river?

   ☐ a. Rappahannock   ☐ b. Chickamauga
   ☐ c. James   ☐ d. Potomac

THE COPPERHEAD PARTY.——IN FAVOR OF *A VIGOROUS PROSECUTION OF PEACE!*

QUIZ 27
TRUE OR FALSE

1. In 1861, more slaves than free people lived in South Carolina.
   ❏ True   ❏ False

2. J.E.B. Stuart was originally commissioned into the Confederate Army as an infantry officer.
   ❏ True   ❏ False

3. In terms of casualties, Gettysburg is the largest battle ever fought in North America.
   ❏ True   ❏ False

DID YOU KNOW...

Newly promoted Lieutenant-General Ulysses S. Grant was almost killed while being photographed. After receiving his promotion, but before he made his first visit to the Army of the Potomac, General Grant stopped by Mathew Brady's photography studio for an official portrait. In order to get better lighting, Brady ordered his assistant to open the skylight in the ceiling above Grant's chair. While attempting to open the window, the assistant put his foot through the glass and sent a shower of razor-sharp shards raining down on Grant. By a stroke of luck, all of the major fragments missed Grant, and he was unharmed. Secretary of War Edwin Stanton, who had accompanied Grant, ordered Brady not to repeat the story for fear that people would interpret it as an assassination attempt.

4. During the war, David Farragut became the first vice admiral of the US Navy.
   ❑ True   ❑ False

5. Texas seceded less than five years after being admitted to the Union.
   ❑ True   ❑ False

6. General George Pickett was not present at the battle of Chancellorsville.
   ❑ True   ❑ False

7. Ulysses S. Grant died of a brain hemorrhage.
   ❑ True   ❑ False

8. William T. Sherman was wounded in the Mexican–American War.
   ❑ True   ❑ False

9. The town of Winchester, Virginia changed hands between the North and the South over 50 times during the course of the war.
   ❑ True   ❑ False

10. Beaver Dam Creek occurred on the fourth day of the Seven Days Battles.
    ❑ True   ❑ False

The plan succeeded. They attacked Sumter, it fell and thus, did more service than it otherwise could.

Abraham Lincoln

QUIZ 28
SHORT ANSWER

EASY

1. In which battle was Patrick Cleburne killed?

. . . .

2. Most members of the "Orphan Brigade" came from which state?

. . . .

3. From what metal was the 12-pounder smoothbore Napoleon cannon cast?

. . . .

4. General John Bell Hood lost the use of which arm at Gettysburg?

. . . .

5. The first Civil War photographs to depict dead soldiers were taken after which battle?

. . . .

6. How many sides did Fort Sumter have?

. . . .

7. Did Edgar Allan Poe die before, after, or during the Civil War?

. . . .

8. Was St John R. Liddell a general for the Union or Confederacy?

. . . .

9. Did Maryland legislators ever vote on secession?

. . . .

10. Which highly literary former Confederate general wrote *Destruction and Reconstruction*, first published in 1879?

. . . .

MULTIPLE CHOICE, "STONEWALL" JACKSON

1. In which branch of the US Army did Jackson fight during the Mexican–American War?

   ☐ a. infantry ☐ b. cavalry
   ☐ c. artillery ☐ d. none of the above

2. What was Jackson's middle name?

   ☐ a. James ☐ b. Joshua
   ☐ c. Joseph ☐ d. Jonathan

3. What rank did Jackson hold in the Confederate Army during the battle of First Bull Run?

   ☐ a. colonel ☐ b. brigadier-general
   ☐ c. lieutenant-general ☐ d. major-general

4. "Jackson of the Chickahominy" is a term used to describe Jackson's performance during which campaign?

   ☐ a. Shenandoah Valley ☐ b. Seven Days Battles
   ☐ c. Second Bull Run ☐ d. Antietam

5. Officially, what killed Jackson?

   ☐ a. pneumonia ☐ b. influenza
   ☐ c. blood loss ☐ d. yellow fever

6. What was the name of Jackson's first wife?

   ☐ a. Susan ☐ b. Eleanor
   ☐ c. Hezekiah ☐ d. Elizabeth

7. Which future Union general was roommates with Jackson in his junior year at West Point?

   ❑ a. Ulysses S. Grant   ❑ b. John Reynolds
   ❑ c. George B. McClellan   ❑ d. George Stoneman

8. Which of these regiments was NOT a part of Jackson's brigade at First Bull Run?

   ❑ a. 2nd Virginia   ❑ b. 4th Virginia
   ❑ c. 5th Virginia   ❑ d. 7th Virginia

9. Which regiment mistakenly fired the shot that struck Jackson down at Chancellorsville?

   ❑ a. 12th North Carolina   ❑ b. 18th North Carolina
   ❑ c. 26th North Carolina   ❑ d. 32nd North Carolina

10. To which Christian church did Jackson belong?

   ❑ a. Methodist   ❑ b. Episcopal
   ❑ c. Baptist   ❑ d. Presbyterian

I had no faith in the sabre as a weapon. I only made the men draw their sabres to prevent them from wasting their fire before they got to closer quarters.

John S. Mosby

MATCH UP

Match these battles with the state in which they were fought.

1. Honey Hill   a) Tennessee

2. Sabine Pass   b) Alabama

3. Wilson's Creek   c) Maryland

4. Champion Hill   d) North Carolina

5. Bentonville   e) Missouri

6. Spanish Fort   f) Mississippi

7. Shiloh   g) Georgia

8. Perryville   h) Kentucky

9. Chickamauga   i) South Carolina

10. South Mountain   j) Texas

QUIZ 31
MULTIPLE CHOICE

1. The 1862 battle of Prairie Grove was fought in which state?

   ❑ a. Missouri   ❑ b. Kentucky
   ❑ c. West Virginia   ❑ d. Arkansas

2. In what year did the Union launch the submarine USS *Alligator*?

   ❑ a. 1861   ❑ b. 1862
   ❑ c. 1863   ❑ d. 1864

3. Admiral David Farragut raised his flag over which ship during the capture of New Orleans?

   ❑ a. USS *Monongahela*   ❑ b. USS *Hartford*
   ❑ c. USS *Richmond*   ❑ d. USS *Albatross*

4. Who led the Union forces at the 1862 battle of Mill Springs?

   ❑ a. George Henry Thomas   ❑ b. Robert Latimer McCook
   ❑ c. Samuel Perry Carter   ❑ d. Ferdinand Van Derveer

5. From which state did "Border Ruffians" usually strike?

   ❑ a. Kansas   ❑ b. Kentucky
   ❑ c. Missouri   ❑ d. Tennessee

6. Which battle was partially lit up by the *aurora borealis*?

   ❑ a. Antietam   ❑ b. Fredericksburg
   ❑ c. Chancellorsville ❑ d. Gettysburg

7. What is the name of the iron corkscrew fitted to a pole that is used to search cannon bores for pieces of the powder bag after firing?

   ❑ a. vent pick   ❑ b. thumbstall
   ❑ c. prolonge   ❑ d. worm

8. Which ship was bought by the "Ladies Gunboat Association of Charleston"?

   ❑ a. CSS *Savannah*   ❑ b. CSS *Georgia*
   ❑ c. CSS *Palmetto State* ❑ d. CSS *Nashville*

9. Who commanded the Union garrison at Knoxville during General Longstreet's attack in 1863?

   ❑ a. Joseph Hooker   ❑ b. Fitz John Porter
   ❑ c. Ambrose Burnside   ❑ d. Don Carlos Buell

10. After his promotion to lieutenant-general, how many stars did Ulysses S. Grant wear on each shoulder?

   ❑ a. 1   ❑ b. 2
   ❑ c. 3   ❑ d. 4

THE REBEL CHIVALRY

As the Fancy of "My Maryland" painted them.   As "My Maryland" found them.

QUIZ 32
TRUE OR FALSE

1. On average, every Confederate general was wounded once.
   ❑ True   ❑ False

2. USS *Kearsarge* had never fired a shot in battle before her encounter with CSS *Alabama*.
   ❑ True   ❑ False

3. Jefferson Davis and Robert E. Lee were in the same class at West Point.
   ❑ True   ❑ False

4. Abraham Lincoln was the first US President from a free state to be re-elected.
   ❑ True   ❑ False

5. John Buford was promoted to major-general after his death in 1863.
   ❑ True   ❑ False

6. Confederate general John B. Gordon attended West Point for two years before dropping out.
   ❑ True   ❑ False

7. Abraham Lincoln was assassinated on Good Friday.
   ❑ True   ❑ False

8. Confederate general John Gregg did not survive the war.
   ❑ True   ❑ False

9. Confederate general Thomas Hindman was mortally wounded at the battle of Kennesaw Mountain.
   ❑ True   ❑ False

10. No battle during the war took place within the city limits of Washington, D.C.
    ❑ True   ❑ False

QUIZ 33
SHORT ANSWER

1. Who was the only Native American to reach the rank of general in either army before Robert E. Lee's surrender?

....

2. Who led the Confederate cavalry on the successful "Beefsteak Raid" in 1864?

....

3. Was the Colt Model 1851 Navy revolver a single-action or double-action weapon?

....

4. What does "Chickamauga" mean?

....

DID YOU KNOW...

In 1859, the future Union general Daniel Sickles discovered his wife was having an affair with Philip Barton Key, the son of Francis Scott Key. Enraged, Sickles found Key and shot him dead just outside the White House. During his trial for murder, Sickles was defended by future Secretary of War, Edwin M. Stanton. Stanton convinced Sickles to plead "temporary insanity," the first time such a plea had ever been heard in an American court. The defense was successful. Sickles was acquitted and, in defiance of social convention, reconciled with his wife.

5. Was the CSS *H.L. Hunley* on the surface or below the water when it struck the USS *Housatonic*?

   ....

6. What was the least populous state to secede from the Union?

   ....

7. Which battle began in 1862 and ended in 1863?

   ....

8. How many Confederates held the rank of Admiral?

   ....

9. What was Joseph E. Johnston's middle name?

   ....

10. Most Cherokee Indians who fought in the war fought for which side?

   ....

I would rather be assassinated than see a single star removed from the American flag.

Abraham Lincoln

QUIZ 34
MULTIPLE CHOICE

1. Approximately how many men comprised Irvin McDowell's army as he marched to the battle of First Manassas?

   ❑ a. 28,000   ❑ b. 35,000
   ❑ c. 42,000   ❑ d. 49,000

2. Which battle contained "The Mule Shoe"?

   ❑ a. Cold Harbor   ❑ b. Fredericksburg
   ❑ c. Second Manassas   ❑ d. Spotsylvania Courthouse

3. Of the following, who is NOT depicted in the rock carving at Stone Mountain?

   ❑ a. Robert E. Lee   ❑ b. James Longstreet
   ❑ c. Thomas J. "Stonewall" ❑ d. Jefferson Davis
       Jackson

4. In what state was the 1864 battle of Marianna?

   ❑ a. Texas   ❑ b. Alabama
   ❑ c. Florida   ❑ d. Virginia

5. Who was "La Belle Rebelle"?

   ❑ a. Maria Boyd   ❑ b. Clara Barton
   ❑ c. Loreta Janeta Valazquez   ❑ d. Mary Otey

6. After Virginia, which state saw more full-scale battles than any other?

- ❑ a. Mississippi
- ❑ b. Tennessee
- ❑ c. West Virginia
- ❑ d. Missouri

7. Who was the only documented civilian casualty of the battle of Gettysburg?

- ❑ a. Jennie Wade
- ❑ b. Lucy Livermore
- ❑ c. Wilfred King
- ❑ d. Susan Codori

8. What was the last state to join the Union before the secession of South Carolina?

- ❑ a. Nevada
- ❑ b. New Mexico
- ❑ c. Kansas
- ❑ d. California

9. In 1861, William F. Ketchum patented what kind of weapon that saw service during the war?

- ❑ a. machine gun
- ❑ b. hand grenade
- ❑ c. man-portable mortar
- ❑ d. steam gun

10. Which of these best defines a "vedette"?

- ❑ a. an artillery fortification
- ❑ b. a mounted sentry
- ❑ c. an anti-infantry obstacle
- ❑ d. a French-made breechloading rifle

ANAGRAMS

"Stew Soft Earth"

(Answers on page 216)

MATCH UP

Match up these famous Civil War books with their authors.

1. *Battle Cry of Freedom*   a) Michael Shara

2. *The Killer Angels*   b) Margaret Mitchell

3. *The Civil War: A Narrative*   c) Irene Hunt

4. *Across Five Aprils*   d) Charles Frazier

5. *"Stonewall" Jackson*   e) James M. McPherson

6. *Red Badge of Courage*   f) Stephen Crane

7. *A Stillness at Appomattox*   g) Douglas Southall Freeman

8. *Gone with the Wind*   h) Bruce Catton

9. *Lee's Lieutenants*   i) Shelby Foote

10. *Cold Mountain*   j) James Robertson

QUIZ 36
FAMOUS FACES

Name these major Civil War figures.

1.

2.

3.

4.

5.

6.

ANSWERS

QUIZ 1 – MULTIPLE CHOICE
1)c 2)a 3)c 4)d 5)b 6)b 7)d 8)b 9)a 10)c

QUIZ 2 – TRUE OR FALSE
1) True
2) True
3) False. Robert E. Lee never smoked
4) True
5) False. Chickamauga saw nearly 5,000 more casualties than Antietam
6) True
7) True. But only as far as Rough and Ready, Georgia
8) False. He held the right
9) False. He was the son of Zachary Taylor
10) False. It was established in 1842

QUIZ 3 – SHORT ANSWER
1) Gideon Wells, Secretary of the Navy
2) Chickamauga
3) The Iron Brigade
4) Gettysburg
5) James Buchanan
6) Slavery
7) 1,000
8) The Confederacy
9) Henry
10) Jefferson Davis

QUIZ 4 – MULTIPLE CHOICE
1)d 2)c 3)a 4)a 5)d 6)a 7)c 8)d 9)c 10)b

QUIZ 5 – MATCH UP
1)f 2)a 3)i 4)j 5)d 6)b 7)h 8)e 9)g 10)c

QUIZ 6 – MULTIPLE CHOICE
1)b 2)a 3)b 4)b 5)c 6)d 7)b 8)a 9)c 10)b

QUIZ 7 – TRUE OR FALSE
1) False
2) False. He graduated second in his class
3) True. Jefferson Columbus Davis
4) False. George Washington also held the rank

5) False. Close to 75 percent survived

6) True

7) False. That nickname was given to Nathan Bedford Forrest

8) False

9) True

10) False. They surrendered under the condition that they would be paroled

QUIZ 8 – SHORT ANSWER

1) Bloody Bill

2) Georgia

3) Hiram Berdan

4) USS *Monitor*

5) Alabama

6) Winfield Scott

7) Edwin M. Stanton

8) Nathan Bedford Forrest

9) Brinton

10) A regiment

QUIZ 9 – MULTIPLE CHOICE, ABRAHAM LINCOLN

1)d 2)c 3)c 4)a 5)d 6)d 7)b 8)a 9)c 10)d

QUIZ 10 – MATCH UP

1)h 2)c 3)f 4)e 5)j 6)g 7)i 8)b 9)a 10)d

QUIZ 11 – MULTIPLE CHOICE

1)d 2)c 3)c 4)b 5)c 6)d 7)c 8)a 9)c 10)a

QUIZ 12 – TRUE OR FALSE

1) False

2) False. There are well over 100

3) False. He was the son of Colonel "Light Horse" Harry Lee

4) True

5) True

6) True

7) True

8) False. He graduated as part of the class of 1837

9) False. Baseball predates the Civil War

10) True. At Bentonville

QUIZ 13 – SHORT ANSWER

1) 35

2) Allan Pinkerton

3) Bottom

4) Paint a log to look like a cannon

5) Stephen R. Mallory

6) Harriet Beecher Stowe

7) Atlanta, Georgia

8) Leonidas Polk

9) Lord Palmerston

10) George Meade

QUIZ 14 – MULTIPLE CHOICE
1)c 2)c 3)b 4)d 5)c 6)b 7)b 8)b 9)a 10)c

QUIZ 15 – MATCH UP
1)d 2)b 3)e 4)f 5)j 6)i 7)h 8)a 9)g 10)c

QUIZ 16 – MULTIPLE CHOICE
1)c 2)d 3)a 4)c 5)b 6)b 7)c 8)d 9)b 10)c

QUIZ 17 – TRUE OR FALSE
1) False. He was wounded multiple times

2) True

3) False. At least a dozen were used on land and on boats

4) True

5) True

6) True

7) False

8) False. He spent two years in prison before being paroled

9) False. It referred to a unit which included infantry, cavalry, and artillery

10) True

QUIZ 18 – SHORT ANSWER
1) Robert Gould Shaw

2) Abner Doubleday

3) Four. Delaware, Maryland, Kentucky, and Missouri

4) Montgomery, Alabama

5) Daniel Sickles

6) The Confederacy

7) Virginia

8) Jubal Anderson Early

9) Sharps rifle

10) The South

QUIZ 19 – MULTIPLE CHOICE, THE VICKSBURG CAMPAIGN
1)b 2)d 3)d 4)d 5)a 6)b 7)a 8)c 9)b 10)b

QUIZ 20 – MATCH UP
1)b 2)i 3)a 4)e 5)j 6)c 7)h 8)d 9)g 10)f

QUIZ 21 – MULTIPLE CHOICE
1)b 2)d 3)b 4)b 5)b 6)a 7)a 8)b 9)b 10)d

QUIZ 22 – TRUE OR FALSE
1) False. Only 16 of the 62 crewmen were lost
2) True
3) True. It is located on the Wilderness battlefield
4) True
5) False. He was captured once during the Peninsula Campaign
6) True. May 3, 1863 which also saw the battles of Second Fredericksburg and Salem Church
7) False. There were none
8) True
9) True. At the end of the war, he led a band into Mexico. He returned two years later and became a farmer
10) True

QUIZ 23 – SHORT ANSWER
1) Benjamin "Spoons" Butler
2) Joshua Chamberlain
3) First Bull Run
4) The Confederacy
5) John Pope
6) Chancellorsville
7) USS *Cumberland*
8) Algeria
9) Stretcher bearers
10) USS *Weehawken*

QUIZ 24 – MULTIPLE CHOICE
1)c 2)d 3)d 4)a 5)c 6)b 7)d 8)b 9)d 10)b

QUIZ 25 – MATCH UP
1)f 2)j 3)c 4)b 5)a 6)g 7)d 8)i 9)h 10)e

QUIZ 26 – MULTIPLE CHOICE
1)a 2)b 3)b 4)c 5)b 6)c 7)a 8)b 9)a 10)c

QUIZ 27 – TRUE OR FALSE

1) True

2) True

3) True

4) True

5) False. It was closer to 15 years

6) True

7) False. He died of throat cancer

8) False. He did not participate in the war

9) True

10) False. It was fought on the second day

QUIZ 28 – SHORT ANSWER

1) Franklin

2) Kentucky

3) Bronze

4) The left

5) Antietam

6) Five

7) Before

8) Confederacy

9) No

10) Richard Taylor

QUIZ 29 – MULTIPLE CHOICE, "STONEWALL" JACKSON

1)c 2)d 3)b 4)b 5)a 6)b 7)d 8)d 9)b 10)d

QUIZ 30 – MATCH UP

1)i 2)j 3)e 4)f 5)d 6)b 7)a 8)h 9)g 10)c

QUIZ 31 – MULTIPLE CHOICE

1)d 2)b 3)b 4)a 5)c 6)b 7)d 8)c 9)c 10)c

QUIZ 32 – TRUE OR FALSE

1) True. Or just about; 49 percent were wounded, on average 1.9 times each

2) True

3) False. Jefferson Davis, class of 1828, was a year ahead of Lee

4) True

5) False. He received notification of his promotion while on his death bed

6) False. He never went to West Point

7) True

8) True. He was killed leading an attack during the siege of Petersburg

9) False. He survived the war only to be assassinated in 1868
10) False. Fort Stevens inside Washington, D.C. came under attack on July 11–12, 1864

QUIZ 33 – SHORT ANSWER
1) Stand Watie
2) Wade Hampton
3) Single-action
4) Literally "stagnant water" although it is often loosely translated as "river of death"
5) On the surface
6) Florida
7) Stone's River (or Murfreesboro)
8) Two. Franklin Buchanan and Raphael Semmes
9) Eggleston
10) The Confederacy

QUIZ 34 – MULTIPLE CHOICE
1)b 2)d 3)b 4)c 5)a 6)b 7)a 8)c 9)b 10)b

QUIZ 35 – MATCH UP
1)e 2)a 3)i 4)c 5)j 6)f 7)h 8)b 9)g 10)d

QUIZ 36 – FAMOUS FACES
1) Leonidas Polk, Confederate general (and bishop)
2) Abner Doubleday, Union general
3) John Hunt Morgan, Confederate cavalry general
4) John F. Reynolds, Union general
5) Albert Sidney Johnston, Confederate general
6) Earl Van Dorn, Confederate general

CHALLENGING
QUESTIONS

TWO-STAR GENERAL
KNOWLEDGE

QUIZ 37
MULTIPLE CHOICE

1. Which of these Confederate generals was NOT a brigade commander in Jackson's Corps during the battle of Antietam?

   ❏ a. Richard Ewell ❏ b. John Bell Hood
   ❏ c. A.P. Hill ❏ d. D.H. Hill

2. In which month was First Manassas fought?

   ❏ a. April ❏ b. May
   ❏ c. June ❏ d. July

3. Which of these battles was NOT fought in Georgia?

   ❏ a. Kennesaw Mountain ❏ b. Ezra Church
   ❏ c. Fort Pulaski ❏ d. Secessionville

4. What was the first double-turreted monitor launched by the US Navy?

   ❏ a. USS *Onondaga* ❏ b. USS *Pensacola*
   ❏ c. USS *Weehawken* ❏ d. USS *Cairo*

5. Which year saw the first United States Income Tax levied?

   ❏ a. 1860 ❏ b. 1861
   ❏ c. 1862 ❏ d. 1863

6. How many hours after the Confederates opened fire on Fort Sumter did it surrender?

   ❏ a. 34 ❏ b. 42
   ❏ c. 54 ❏ d. 66

7. How many guns made up an artillery "section"?

☐ a. 2   ☐ b. 6

☐ c. 12   ☐ d. 24

8. Which of these ships, commanded by Thomas O. Selfridge, was NOT sunk during the war?

☐ a. USS *Cumberland*   ☐ b. USS *Conestoga*

☐ c. USS *Cairo*   ☐ d. USS *Huron*

9. Which of these best defines a "shebang"?

☐ a. narrow log bridge

☐ b. crude weather shelter

☐ c. litter for carrying the wounded

☐ d. observation tower

10. What type of equipment was a "brogan"?

☐ a. shirt   ☐ b. pants

☐ c. shoe   ☐ d. hat

DID YOU KNOW...

After illegally capturing the CSS *Florida* in a neutral Brazilian port, Commander Napoleon Collins towed his prize back to the United States. Although glad to be rid of the notorious Confederate commerce raider, Secretary of State William Seward expressed regret that the ship wasn't sunk as she would likely have to be returned to Brazil. A few days later, the captured *Florida* "accidently" rammed into another ship and sank.

QUIZ 38
TRUE OR FALSE

1. Early in the war, William T. Sherman outranked Ulysses S. Grant.
   ❑ True   ❑ False

2. After the war, former US Vice-President and Confederate general John C. Breckinridge fled the United States never to return.
   ❑ True   ❑ False

3. Confederate general Patrick Cleburne had served in the British Army.
   ❑ True   ❑ False

4. Over 30 percent of all Confederate generals were killed or mortally wounded in combat.
   ❑ True   ❑ False

"MASTERLY INACTIVITY," OR SIX MONTHS ON THE POTOMAC.

5. Nathan Bedford Forrest attempted to disband the Ku Klux Klan because he thought its violence had gotten out of hand.

   ❑ True   ❑ False

6. Sam Houston was governor of Texas when it seceded from the Union.

   ❑ True   ❑ False

7. During the war, control of the United States Marine Corps was turned over to the US Army.

   ❑ True   ❑ False

8. Nearly 10,000 men from North Carolina fought for the Union.

   ❑ True   ❑ False

9. The CSS *H.L. Hunley* was the only Confederate submarine to attack a US Navy vessel.

   ❑ True   ❑ False

10. Abraham Lincoln had never seen a show at Ford's Theater before the night of his assassination.

   ❑ True   ❑ False

If I could save the Union without freeing any slave, I would do it; and if I could save it by freeing all the slaves, I would do it; and if I could save it by freeing some and leaving others alone, I would do that.

Abraham Lincoln

QUIZ 39
SHORT ANSWER

1. Which side suffered more casualties at the battle of Stone's River, the North or the South?

   . . . .

2. What term did the US Army use to describe all of the horses, equipment, and men assigned to operate one piece of field artillery?

   . . . .

3. Was George A. Custer promoted to brigadier-general before or after the battle of Gettysburg?

   . . . .

4. Who was the publisher of the *North Star* newspaper, which was later renamed in his honor?

   . . . .

5. Which Confederate general was known to some of his men as "Damn Born"?

   . . . .

6. What was the first National Military Park in the United States?

   . . . .

7. What is the second half of this line from *The Battle Hymn of the Republic*: "He is trampling out the vintage…"

   . . . .

8. What nickname did Confederate soldier Richard Rowland Kirkland acquire during the battle of Fredericksburg?

   . . . .

9. Which political party ceased to exist just before the Civil War, primarily because of a dispute about slavery?

. . . .

10. What piece of common campaign equipment did Civil War soldiers often refer to as a "housewife"?

. . . .

© Simon Tofield

QUIZ 40
MULTIPLE CHOICE, CIVIL WAR MOVIES

1. Which of the following actors did NOT appear in the 1989 movie *Glory*?

   ❑ a. Denzel Washington   ❑ b. Samuel L. Jackson
   ❑ c. Andre Braugher   ❑ d. Morgan Freeman

2. In which year did the movie *Gone with the Wind* premiere in Atlanta?

   ❑ a. 1933   ❑ b. 1936
   ❑ c. 1939   ❑ d. 1942

3. Who directed the 1999 movie *Ride with the Devil*?

   ❑ a. Ang Lee   ❑ b. Sam Rami
   ❑ c. Ridley Scott   ❑ d. Roland Emmerich

4. Who played the role of General James Longstreet in the 2003 movie *Gods and Generals*?

   ❑ a. Bill Campbell   ❑ b. Patrick Gorman
   ❑ c. Tom Berenger   ❑ d. Bruce Boxleitner

5. Who played the lead role of Henry Flemming in the 1951 movie *The Red Badge of Courage*?

   ❑ a. Bill Mauldin   ❑ b. Rock Hudson
   ❑ c. Audie Murphy   ❑ d. Andy Devin

6. What is the name of Patrick Swayze's character in the 1985 miniseries *North & South*?

   ❑ a. George Hazard ❑ b. Patrick Flynn
   ❑ c. Justine LaMotte ❑ d. Orry Main

7. The 1993 movie *Gettysburg* is based on which book?

   ❑ a. *Pickett's Charge* ❑ b. *Plenty of Blame to Go Around*
   ❑ c. *The Days at Gettysburg* ❑ d. *The Killer Angels*

8. The 1959 movie *The Horse Soldiers* presented a highly fictionalized account of a cavalry raid led by which commander?

   ❑ a. John Hunt Morgan ❑ b. J.E.B. Stuart
   ❑ c. Benjamin Grierson ❑ d. Joseph Shelby

9. The 1915 movie *Birth of a Nation* is based on which book?

   ❑ a. *The Clansman* ❑ b. *The Challenge to Sirius*
   ❑ c. *So Red the Rose* ❑ d. *Long Remember*

10. In which state would you find "Cold Mountain," the setting for the movie and the book of the same name?

   ❑ a. Georgia ❑ b. South Carolina
   ❑ c. North Carolina ❑ d. Virginia

War is cruelty. There is no use trying to reform it. The crueller it is, the sooner it will be over.

William T. Sherman

QUIZ 41
MATCH UP

Match these Union generals with an Army they commanded.

1. Gordon Granger   a) Army of the Gulf

2. Edward Canby   b) Army of the Cumberland

3. Philip Sheridan   c) Army of the James

4. Don Carlos Buell   d) Army of the Ohio

5. George B. McClellan   e) Army of the Mississippi

6. Henry Slocum   f) Army of the Potomac

7. George Henry Thomas   g) Army of Virginia

8. John Pope   h) Army of Kentucky

9. Edward O.C. Ord   i) Army of the Shenendoah

10. John A. McClernand   j) Army of Georgia

QUIZ 42
MULTIPLE CHOICE

1. Confederate general Wade Hampton was born in which state?

   ❑ a. Virginia   ❑ b. North Carolina
   ❑ c. South Carolina   ❑ d. Mississippi

2. Which of these was NOT a Union army during the war?

   ❑ a. Army of the James   ❑ b. Army of East Tennessee
   ❑ c. Army of West Virginia   ❑ d. Army of the Mountain
                                                 Department

3. Who was the first US officer to be promoted to lieutenant-general during the war?

   ❑ a. George B. McClellan   ❑ b. Ulysses S. Grant
   ❑ c. Joseph Hooker   ❑ d. George Meade

4. Which constitutional amendment outlawed slavery?

   ❑ a. 11th   ❑ b. 12th
   ❑ c. 13th   ❑ d. 14th

5. Who was second-in-command of the Army of the Potomac during the battle of Chancellorsville?

   ❑ a. Darius Couch   ❑ b. George Meade
   ❑ c. Philip Sheridan   ❑ d. Henry Chipman

6. In which year was the battle of Allatoona Pass fought?

   ❑ a. 1861   ❑ b. 1862
   ❑ c. 1863   ❑ d. 1864

7. Where was the "last Capital of the Confederacy"?

   ☐ a. Danville, VA   ☐ b. Greensboro, NC
   ☐ c. Columbia, SC   ☐ d. Montgomery, AL

8. Who was the first Union general killed during the war?

   ☐ a. William Grose   ☐ b. Robert C. Scheneck
   ☐ c. Truman Seymor   ☐ d. Nathaniel Lyon

9. Who was appointed to command of the Army of Tennessee upon Braxton Bragg's removal in 1863?

   ☐ a. John C. Breckinridge   ☐ b. Benjamin F. Cheatham
   ☐ c. Joseph E. Johnston   ☐ d. William Hardee

10. In what year was the first official Thanksgiving celebrated?

   ☐ a. 1862   ☐ b. 1863
   ☐ c. 1864   ☐ d. 1865

DID YOU KNOW...

In late 1864, General Benjamin Butler stood before the Joint Congressional Committee on the Conduct of the War and argued that he had been unfairly dismissed from his command after his failure to capture Fort Fisher. He stated that the defenses of Fort Fisher were impregnable. Just then, in the middle of Butler's defense, a cry went up from outside the building. The newspapers had announced the capture of Fort Fisher. Benjamin Butler joined in the laughter and was later cleared of any misconduct.

QUIZ 43
TRUE OR FALSE

1. The US Marine Corps never numbered more than 5,000 officers and men during the war.
   ❏ True   ❏ False

2. General James Longstreet helped man a cannon during the battle of Antietam.
   ❏ True   ❏ False

3. Mathew Brady was hired by the US government in 1862 to follow and photograph the Army of the Potomac.
   ❏ True   ❏ False

4. Robert E. Lee and James Longstreet never met again after 1865.
   ❏ True   ❏ False

5. Fewer than half of the colored regiments raised during the war actually saw combat.
   ❏ True   ❏ False

THE BLOCKADE ON THE "CONNECTICUT PLAN".

6. John S. Mosby surrendered his command a week after Lee surrendered at Appomattox.
   ❑ True   ❑ False

7. A majority of the participants in the battle of Honey Springs were either Native American or African-American.
   ❑ True   ❑ False

8. George Pickett was never wounded during the war.
   ❑ True   ❑ False

9. More people died in the American Civil War than all of the French Revolutionary and Napoleonic Wars 1792–1815.
   ❑ True   ❑ False

10. Just over half of all West Point graduates serving in the US Army in 1860 resigned their commissions to serve the South.
    ❑ True   ❑ False

DID YOU KNOW...

During the fight for "Bloody Lane" at the battle of Antietam, Confederate general John B. Gordon was wounded five times. His fifth wound was a shot in the face that rendered him unconscious. He collapsed face-downward and was only saved from drowning in his own blood due to a hole in his hat.

SHORT ANSWER

1. According to the Constitution of the Confederacy, how long was a Presidential term in office?

   . . . .

2. With what name did the Confederacy rechristen the *Sea King* after purchasing the ship in 1864?

   . . . .

3. A "Stand of Arms" contained how many rifles or muskets?

   . . . .

4. Who succeeded J.E.B. Stuart as head of the cavalry of the Army of Northern Virginia?

   . . . .

5. What was a "Sherman's Necktie"?

   . . . .

6. Which Civil War veteran wrote *The Devil's Dictionary*?

   . . . .

7. What was the most populous city in the Confederacy?

   . . . .

8. What caliber was the United States Rifle Musket, Model 1861?

   . . . .

9. What was the highest numbered corps in the Union Army during the war?

   . . . .

10. Which river did Fort Donelson guard?

    . . . .

QUIZ 45
MULTIPLE CHOICE

1. What US Army rank did Robert E. Lee hold when he resigned his commission in 1861?

    ❑ a. major   ❑ b. lieutenant-colonel
    ❑ c. colonel   ❑ d. brigadier-general

2. Which was the largest Union Army to participate in the Atlanta campaign?

    ❑ a. Army of the Cumberland
    ❑ b. Army of the Tennessee
    ❑ c. Army of the Mississippi
    ❑ d. Army of the Ohio

3. Who was the second man to command the "Stonewall Brigade"?

    ❑ a. James A. Walker   ❑ b. Richard B. Garnett
    ❑ c. Andrew J. Birbsby   ❑ d. Elish F. Paxton

4. What caliber is a Sharps rifle?

    ❑ a. .22   ❑ b. .32
    ❑ c. .44   ❑ d. .52

5. Who commanded the left wing of Sherman's command (also known as the Army of Georgia) during the March to the Sea?

    ❑ a. Henry W. Slocum   ❑ b. Alpheus S. Williams
    ❑ c. Oliver O. Howard   ❑ d. John A. Logan

6. In what year was the battle of Tupelo?

    ❑ a. 1862   ❑ b. 1863
    ❑ c. 1864   ❑ d. 1865

7. Where was President Andrew Johnson born?

    ❑ a. Baltimore, MD   ❑ b. Charlotte, NC
    ❑ c. Raleigh, NC   ❑ d. Lexington, VA

8. How many men did a full artillery platoon contain?

    ❑ a. 6   ❑ b. 8
    ❑ c. 16   ❑ d. 32

9. From which university was John S. Mosby expelled for shooting a fellow student?

    ❑ a. University of Virginia   ❑ b. Washington University
    ❑ c. West Point   ❑ d. Virginia Military Institute

10. In which year did the United States Supreme Court make its "Dread Scott Decision"?

    ❑ a. 1850   ❑ b. 1853
    ❑ c. 1857   ❑ d. 1859

ANAGRAMS

"Hedge Within Town"

(Answers on page 216)

MATCH UP

Match these battles with the victorious army commander.

1. Chickamauga

a) Samuel R. Curtis

2. Big Bethel

b) John B. Magruder

3. Roanoke Island

c) Ulysses S. Grant

4. Port Republic

d) George H. Thomas

5. Pea Ridge

e) P.G.T. Beauregard

6. Chattanooga

f) Ambrose Burnside

7. Monocacy

g) Willliam T. Sherman

8. Nashville

h) Thomas J. "Stonewall" Jackson

9. Bentonvillle

i) Braxton Bragg

10. Fort Sumter

j) Jubal Early

QUIZ 47

MULTIPLE CHOICE

CHALLENGING

1. Which Union general acquired the nickname "The Rock of Chickamauga"?

   ❑ a. George H. Thomas ❑ b. John M. Schofield
   ❑ c. Henry W. Slocum ❑ d. Oliver O. Howard

2. How old was George A. Custer when he was promoted to brigadier-general?

   ❑ a. 21 ❑ b. 23
   ❑ c. 25 ❑ d. 27

3. In which battle did Confederate general Richard Ewell receive the terrible wound that cost him his leg?

   ❑ a. South Mountain ❑ b. Glendale
   ❑ c. Groveton ❑ d. Savage Station

4. To which future Confederate general did Zachory Taylor supposedly say "Double-shot those guns and give 'em hell"?

   ❑ a. Joseph E. Johnston ❑ b. Braxton Bragg
   ❑ c. Thomas J. "Stonewall" ❑ d. Jubal Early
   Jackson

5. How many men were killed in the CSS *H.L. Hunley* when it sank in 1864?

   ❑ a. 2 ❑ b. 4
   ❑ c. 6 ❑ d. 8

6. In which state was Fort Wagner?

☐ a. Virginia   ☐ b. South Carolina
☐ c. North Carolina   ☐ d. Tennessee

7. What was the last battle of Jackson's "Valley Campaign"?

☐ a. Port Republic   ☐ b. Cross Keys
☐ c. Winchester   ☐ d. Front Royal

8. Which Union general was the first to command the officers of his division to wear identifying patches on their caps?

☐ a. Darius Couch   ☐ b. Samuel Curtis
☐ c. Philip Kearny   ☐ d. Henry Slocum

9. Who assumed command of the Confederate Army at the battle of Seven Pines in the *immediate* aftermath of the wounding of Joseph E. Johnston?

☐ a. James Longstreet   ☐ b. Jubal Early
☐ c. J.E.B. Stuart   ☐ d. Gustavus W. Smith

10. Which commander of the Army of the Potomac was born in Cadiz, Spain?

☐ a. George B. McClellan   ☐ b. Irvin McDowell
☐ c. John Pope   ☐ d. George Meade

QUIZ 48

TRUE OR FALSE

1. Despite the formation of many Negro Regiments in the US Army, the US Navy continued to employ only whites until after the war.
   ❑ True ❑ False

2. General Sherman ordered the burning of Columbia, South Carolina.
   ❑ True ❑ False

3. Mathew Brady was present at the battle of First Manassas.
   ❑ True ❑ False

4. Most African-Americans who fought in the Union Army came from Confederate states.
   ❑ True ❑ False

5. The Army of the Potomac had no 6-pounder guns at the battle of Antietam.
   ❑ True ❑ False

6. No colored troops were awarded the Medal of Honor during the war.
   ❑ True ❑ False

7. The 13th Amendment to the Constitution was ratified more than 60 years after the 12th Amendment.
   ❑ True ❑ False

8. Frederick Douglas married a white woman.
   ❑ True ❑ False

9. Less than four years after the firing on Fort Sumter, Charleston, it was occupied by Union soldiers.
   ❑ True ❑ False

10. Ulysses S. Grant never owned slaves.
    ❑ True ❑ False

SHORT ANSWER

1. Which escaped slave was known as "The Moses of her people"?

   . . . .

2. Who was the highest-ranking Confederate to become a "skalawag"?

   . . . .

3. What color were General James Longstreet's eyes?

   . . . .

4. The French invasion of Mexico during the war was a violation of what American foreign-policy doctrine?

   . . . .

5. During the war Confederate general and Episcopal bishop, Leonidas Polk, baptized which two fellow generals?

   . . . .

6. Did the "Laurel Brigade" fight for the Union or the Confederacy?

   . . . .

7. What were the only two Confederate state capitals never captured by the Union Army?

   . . . .

There are times when a corps commander's life does not count.

Winfield S. Hancock at Gettysburg

8. Albert Sidney Johnston fought in the armies of the United States, the Confederate States, and which other nation state?

. . . .

9. Which battle was fought first, Antietam or Iuka?

. . . .

10. "Whatisit"?

. . . .

CHALLENGING

The too Confiding South DRAFTING TERMS OF PEACE with the Federal Government.
(See *Richmond Papers*, July 6, 7, 8.)

MULTIPLE CHOICE, THE BATTLE OF MOBILE BAY

1. Which Confederate ironclad was destroyed during the battle?

   ❏ a. CSS *Richmond*   ❏ b. CSS *Texas*
   ❏ c. CSS *Tennessee*   ❏ d. CSS *Albemarle*

2. Fort Gains sat upon which island?

   ❏ a. Pelican Island   ❏ b. Cedar Island
   ❏ c. Gains Island   ❏ d. Dauphin Island

3. Who led the Union land attack against Fort Gains?

   ❏ a. Gordon Granger   ❏ b. Charles Russell
   ❏ c. John Madill   ❏ d. Thomas Davies

4. Which of the following was NOT a Confederate gunboat that participated in the battle?

   ❏ a. CSS *Morgan*   ❏ b. CSS *Gains*
   ❏ c. CSS *Buchanan*   ❏ d. CSS *Selma*

5. Which Union ironclad struck a torpedo and sank during the battle?

   ❏ a. USS *Manhattan*   ❏ b. USS *Tecumseh*
   ❏ c. USS *Chickasaw*   ❏ d. USS *Winnebago*

6. Which Union ship led the line of wooden ships into the bay?

   ❏ a. USS *Brooklyn*   ❏ b. USS *Lackawanna*
   ❏ c. USS *Ossipee*   ❏ d. USS *Richmond*

7. Who held overall command of the Confederate naval forces during the battle?

   ❑ a. Percival Drayton   ❑ b. Franklin Buchanan
   ❑ c. Tunis Craven   ❑ d. Morgan Johnson

8. Which Confederate officer surrendered Fort Morgan?

   ❑ a. Dabney Maury   ❑ b. James Williams
   ❑ c. Gabriel Rains   ❑ d. Richard Page

9. Which ship served as Admiral David Farragut's flagship during the battle?

   ❑ a. USS *Monongahela*   ❑ b. USS *Hartford*
   ❑ c. USS *Metacomet*   ❑ d. USS *Oneida*

10. The four Confederate vessels that participated had a combined barrage of how many guns?

    ❑ a. 22   ❑ b. 32
    ❑ c. 46   ❑ d. 54

DID YOU KNOW...

John Clem became the youngest ever noncommissioned officer in the US Army when he was promoted to sergeant at the age of 13. Originally enlisting as a nine-year-old drummer boy in the 22nd Michigan, he supposedly earned his promotion by fighting valiantly with a shortened musket at the battle of Chickamauga. Clem would eventually retire from the Army on the eve of World War I with the rank of major-general. He was the last Civil War veteran to serve in the US Army.

QUIZ 51
MATCH UP

Match up these Civil War commanders with their nicknames.

1. Raphael Semmes   a) Old Billy Fixin'

2. Cadmus Marcellus Wilcox   b) The black-bearded Cossack

3. Robert E. Lee   c) Slow Trot

4. Earl Van Dorn   d) Grumble

5. Edward Johnson   e) Buck

6. George H. Thomas   f) Rip

7. Sterling Price   g) Old Pap

8. Eugene A. Carr   h) The Ace of Spades

9. William Jones   i) Allegheny

10. John Salmon Ford   j) Old Beeswax

MULTIPLE CHOICE

1. According to US Army regulations, how many sets of colors was a standard regiment supposed to carry?

   ❏ a. 0   ❏ b. 1
   ❏ c. 2   ❏ d. 3

2. In which battle was the "gallant" Major John Pelham killed?

   ❏ a. Fredericksburg   ❏ b. Kelly's Ford
   ❏ c. Brandy Station   ❏ d. Yellow Tavern

3. In the Confederate Army, what was the lowest-ranking infantry officer officially allowed to keep horses?

   ❏ a. lieutenant   ❏ b. captain
   ❏ c. major   ❏ d. lieutenant-colonel

4. Who was George B. McClellan's running mate in the 1864 election?

   ❏ a. Horatio Seymore   ❏ b. Clement L. Vallandigham
   ❏ c. George H. Pendleton   ❏ d. Henry J. Raymond

5. Who was Commandant of the Confederate States Marine Corps?

   ❏ a. Lloyd Beall   ❏ b. Richard Hawes
   ❏ c. James Rains   ❏ d. Frederick Townsend

No damn man kills me and lives.

Nathan Bedford Forrest

6. USS *Wachusett* violated the neutrality of which country to capture the CSS *Florida*?

   ❑ a. Britain   ❑ b. Spain
   ❑ c. Mexico   ❑ d. Brazil

7. Which of these battles was fought first?

   ❑ a. Antietam   ❑ b. Shiloh
   ❑ c. Wilson's Creek   ❑ d. Perryville

8. Prior to 1863, US Cavalry regiments included a "supernumerary" officer equal to what rank?

   ❑ a. lieutenant   ❑ b. captain
   ❑ c. major   ❑ d. lieutenant-colonel

9. After the war, Ambrose Burnside served two terms as governor of which state?

   ❑ a. Connecticut   ❑ b. New Hampshire
   ❑ c. Rhode Island   ❑ d. Delaware

10. In which state did the 1862 battle of Wood Lake take place?

   ❑ a. Minnesota   ❑ b. Michigan
   ❑ c. South Dakota   ❑ d. North Dakota

Never take counsel of your fears.

Thomas J. "Stonewall" Jackson

QUIZ 53
TRUE OR FALSE

1. Confederate general Edward P. Alexander finished last in his class at West Point.
    ❑ True   ❑ False

2. Ulysses S. Grant and Abraham Lincoln first met during the war.
    ❑ True   ❑ False

3. The Emancipation Proclamation did not apply to Tennessee.
    ❑ True   ❑ False

4. George Dewey, later Admiral Dewey of Manila Bay fame, served during the Civil War.
    ❑ True   ❑ False

5. Joshua Chamberlain lived to see the start of World War I.
    ❑ True   ❑ False

6. The Civil War was the first war in which the telegraph was used.
    ❑ True   ❑ False

7. "Fighting Joe" Wheeler was only 5ft 2in.
    ❑ True   ❑ False

8. Confederate general Edmund Kirby Smith was shot in the neck during First Bull Run.
    ❑ True   ❑ False

9. James Longstreet served as a pallbearer for "Stonewall" Jackson.
    ❑ True   ❑ False

10. The Pony Express began operating within days of First Bull Run.
    ❑ True   ❑ False

QUIZ 54

SHORT ANSWER

1. Did Union general Edwin Vose Sumner serve in the regular army before the war?

. . . .

2. Who wrote *The Battle Hymn of the Republic*?

. . . .

3. In the US Army, which type of sergeant wore a star above his chevrons?

. . . .

4. Who was the Principal Chief of the Western Cherokee who remained neutral throughout the war?

. . . .

THE COPPERHEAD PLAN FOR SUBJUGATING THE SOUTH

War and Argument—Cold Steel and Cool Reason—having failed to restore the Union, it is supposed that the South may be *bored* into coming back.

Our Picture represents the successful operation of this exceedingly humane and ingenious device.

5. What was the only book allowed to Jefferson Davis in his first several months of imprisonment after the war?

. . . .

6. What was James B. McPherson's middle name?

. . . .

7. Fort Wagner was situated on which island?

. . . .

8. In what state was the Johnson's Island prisoner-of-war camp?

. . . .

9. Who was the only other Confederate in the room with Robert E. Lee when he officially surrendered at Appomattox?

. . . .

10. What position did Jonathan Letterman hold in the Army of the Potomac during the battle of Gettysburg?

. . . .

DID YOU KNOW...

The Washington Monument sat half-completed for the duration of the war. Construction of the monument began in 1848 but was halted in 1856 due to a lack of funds. Construction wasn't restarted until 1876 and the monument was finally completed in 1884.

QUIZ 55
MULTIPLE CHOICE

1. In which year was Robert E. Lee appointed as superintendent of West Point?

   ❑ a. 1848   ❑ b. 1852
   ❑ c. 1856   ❑ d. 1859

2. In which battle did Union general Daniel Sickles receive the wound that cost him his leg?

   ❑ a. Antietam   ❑ b. Gettysburg
   ❑ c. the Wilderness   ❑ d. Spotsylvania Courthouse

3. Who surrendered Port Hudson to Nathaniel P. Banks?

   ❑ a. Franklin Gardner ❑ b. Theodore Brevard
   ❑ c. William Smith   ❑ d. Israel Richardson

4. Richmond's 37,000 residents in 1860 put it where in a ranking of the Confederacy's largest cities?

   ❑ a. 1st   ❑ b. 2nd
   ❑ c. 3rd   ❑ d. 8th

5. Which of these battles was NOT fought in Arkansas?

   ❑ a. Arkansas Post ❑ b. Prairie Grove
   ❑ c. Pea Ridge   ❑ d. Spanish Fort

6. Who was the "Black Knight of the Confederacy"?

   ❑ a. Turner Ashby   ❑ b. John S. Mosby
   ❑ c. Nathan Bedford Forrest ❑ d. John Hunt Morgan

7. What year is generally given as the end of "Reconstruction"?

☐ a. 1869   ☐ b. 1877
☐ c. 1882   ☐ d. 1889

8. Which Union general inadvertently invented newspaper "by-lines" when he demanded that all stories sent from the Army be signed?

☐ a. George B. McClellan   ☐ b. Joseph Hooker
☐ c. Ambrose Burnside   ☐ d. George Meade

9. Which of these events occurred last, chronologically?

☐ a. the secession of Florida
☐ b. the firing on Fort Sumter
☐ c. the secession of Georgia
☐ d. the secession of Alabama

10. During the war, how many stars flew on the state flag of Florida?

☐ a. 0   ☐ b. 1
☐ d. 5   ☐ c. 13

ANAGRAMS

"Mixes Land Onion"

(Answers on page 216)

QUIZ 56
MATCH UP

Match these Confederate generals with an Army they commanded.

1. Simon B. Buckner   a) Army of Missouri

2. John C. Pemberton   b) Army of Central Kentucky

3. Robert S. Garnett   c) Army of the Valley

4. Sterling Price   d) Army of the Peninsula

5. D.H. Hill   e) Army of the West

6. Henry H. Sibley   f) Army of the Northwest

7. John B. Magruder   g) Army of Tennessee

8. Jubal Early   h) Army of the Kanawha

9. John P. McCown   i) Army of Mississippi

10. Henry A. Wise   j) Army of New Mexico

QUIZ 57
MULTIPLE CHOICE

1. During which battle did General John Sedgwick supposedly utter his famous last words, "They couldn't hit an elephant at this distance"?

    ❏ a. Antietam   ❏ b. Glendale
    ❏ c. Gettysburg   ❏ d. Spotsylvania Courthouse

2. In which battle was Union colonel and Oregon senator Edward Baker killed?

    ❏ a. Big Bethel   ❏ b. Ball's Bluff
    ❏ c. Cedar Mountain   ❏ d. Five Forks

3. In which state is Fort Pulaski?

    ❏ a. Virginia   ❏ b. North Carolina
    ❏ c. South Carolina   ❏ d. Georgia

4. In the US Army a surgeon was equivalent to what rank?

    ❏ a. lieutenant   ❏ b. captain
    ❏ c. major   ❏ d. lieutenant-colonel

5. Which of the following was NOT one of Professor Thaddeus Lowe's Union observation balloons?

    ❏ a. *Intrepid*   ❏ b. *Washington*
    ❏ c. *Constitution*   ❏ d. *Constellation*

6. Who held command of I Corps of the Union Army during the battle of Antietam?

❑ a. Joseph Hooker ❑ b. John Sedgwick
❑ c. Ambrose Burnside ❑ d. George Meade

7. How old was Jefferson Davis when Mississippi seceded?

❑ a. 48 ❑ b. 50
❑ c. 52 ❑ d. 54

8. Approximately how many men were killed in the fighting during the battle of First Manassas?

❑ a. 300 ❑ b. 800
❑ c. 1,200 ❑ d. 1,800

9. Having graduated from West Point, Robert E. Lee was initially commissioned into which branch of the service?

❑ a. engineers ❑ b. cavalry
❑ c. artillery ❑ d. infantry

10. In which battle did Union infantry make a stand near Snodgrass House?

❑ a. Chattanooga ❑ b. Chickamauga
❑ c. Stone's River ❑ d. Perryville

If I commit an error I do it without bad intention. My great crime in the world is blunder, I will get into scrapes without intention or any bad motive.

Stand Watie

QUIZ 58
TRUE OR FALSE

1. Joshua Chamberlain was wounded so badly during the siege of Petersburg that some newspapers printed his obituary.
   ❑ True   ❑ False

2. Fitz John Porter was dismissed from the Army during the war and not reinstated until after his death.
   ❑ True   ❑ False

3. At one point, the Union hot-air balloon fleet consisted of a dozen balloons.
   ❑ True   ❑ False

4. George B. McClellan remained a general in the US Army during most of his 1864 presidential campaign.
   ❑ True   ❑ False

5. William C. Quantrill never reached a rank higher than captain in Confederate service.
   ❑ True   ❑ False

6. President Lincoln and General Grant first met in late 1863.
   ❑ True   ❑ False

7. By the end of the war, Nathan Bedford Forrest had refused to fight under the command of both General Joseph Wheeler and General Braxton Bragg.
   ❑ True   ❑ False

8. Neither the Union nor the Confederacy had a general whose surname began with "X."
   ❑ True   ❑ False

9. All of the Union volunteers who participated in the Andrews Raid (the Great Locomotive Chase) received the Medal of Honor.

  ❏ True   ❏ False

10. More Americans became casualties during the battle of Shiloh than during the entire American War of Independence.

  ❏ True   ❏ False

© Simon Tofield

QUIZ 59
SHORT ANSWER

1. How many Union generals went on to become President of the United States?

   ....

2. What was a "Galvanized Yankee"?

   ....

3. Which leg did General John Bell Hood lose as a result of his wound during the battle of Chickamauga?

   ....

4. Which future Confederate general broke a plate over the head of Jubal Early at West Point?

   ....

5. Who passed away first, Robert E. Lee or his famous horse, Traveller?

   ....

DID YOU KNOW...

Most Confederate Army hospitals were assigned to treat wounded soldiers from a specific state, as it was believed that mixing soldiers from different states was detrimental to the healing process.

6. Who was Vice-President of the Confederacy?

. . . .

7. What was the "snake-like" name sometimes applied to Peace Democrats?

. . . .

8. Who was the Confederacy's "Prince of Privateers"?

. . . .

9. On what date did the Emancipation Proclamation come into effect?

. . . .

10. Did William Clark Quantrill die before or after the end of the war?

. . . .

A chicken could not live on that field when we open on it.

Edward P. Alexander, commander of Longstreet's artillery battalion, at Fredericksburg

QUIZ 60
MULTIPLE CHOICE, THE LINCOLN ASSASSINATION

1. What play was Lincoln watching when he was killed?

   ❑ a. *The Marble Heart* ❑ b. *Our American Cousin*
   ❑ c. *Franchon the Cricket* ❑ d. *The Merry Wives of Windsor*

2. Who was the play's leading lady, who would later hold the President's bleeding head in her lap?

   ❑ a. Clara Harris ❑ b. Laura Keene
   ❑ c. Charlotte Cushman ❑ d. Ellen Terry

3. Who was the only other man sitting in the Presidential box in Ford's Theater at the time of the assassination?

   ❑ a. John Hay ❑ b. Henry Rathbone
   ❑ c. Isham Haynie ❑ d. Richard Oglesby

4. Who was the first doctor to reach Lincoln after he had been shot?

   ❑ a. Joseph Barnes ❑ b. Edwin Samuel Gaillard
   ❑ c. Charles Leale ❑ d. Josiah Pearce Cannon

5. Which other member of Lincoln's cabinet was also assaulted the night of the President's shooting?

   ❑ a. Secretary of the Navy ❑ b. Secretary of War
   ❑ c. Secretary of State ❑ d. Postmaster General

6. What type of pistol did John Wilkes Booth fire at Lincoln?

- ❑ a. Derringer
- ❑ b. Colt
- ❑ c. LeMat
- ❑ d. Smith & Wesson

7. How many people were eventually hanged for conspiring to assassinate Abraham Lincoln?

- ❑ a. 1
- ❑ b. 2
- ❑ c. 3
- ❑ d. 4

8. Who killed John Wilkes Booth?

- ❑ a. Boston Corbett
- ❑ b. Duncan Kenner
- ❑ c. Horace Neide
- ❑ d. Richard Terry

9. Where was John Wilkes Booth born?

- ❑ a. Montgomery, AL
- ❑ b. Bel Air, MD
- ❑ c. Harpers Ferry, MD
- ❑ d. Danville, VA

10. Who was Lincoln's self-appointed bodyguard who had been sent to Richmond on the night of the assassination?

- ❑ a. Allan Pinkerton
- ❑ b. Ward Hill Lamon
- ❑ c. Henry F. Campbell
- ❑ d. Nathan Ryno Smoth

War loses a great deal of romance after a soldier has seen his first battle. I have a more vivid recollection of the first than the last one I was in. It is a classical maxim that it is sweet and becoming to die for one's country; but whoever has seen the horrors of a battle-field feels that it is far sweeter to live for it.

John S. Mosby

QUIZ 61
MATCH UP

Match these ships with the captains who commanded them in battle.

1. USS *Hatteras*   a) Franklin Buchanan

2. USS *Wachusett*   b) John Newland Maffitt

3. USS *Housatonic*   c) Charles Pickering

4. USS *Weehawken*   d) Napoleon Collins

5. USS *Essex*   e) William A. Webb

6. CSS *Virginia*   f) William D. Porter

7. CSS *Atlanta*   g) Henry T. Blake

8. CSS *Albemarle*   h) George E. Dixon

9. CSS *Florida*   i) James W. Cooke

10. CSS *H.L. Hunley*   j) John Rodgers

QUIZ 62
MULTIPLE CHOICE

1. In which state did the 1861 "Camp Jackson Massacre" occur?

   ❑ a. Kentucky   ❑ b. Tennessee
   ❑ c. Missouri   ❑ d. West Virginia

2. Who took command of I Corp of the Army of Northern Virginia on May 7, 1864 after the wounding of General James Longstreet?

   ❑ a. Richard Anderson   ❑ b. Jubal Early
   ❑ c. John B. Gordon   ❑ d. John Kershaw

3. Which Massachusetts regiment was attacked by a pro-Southern mob as it passed through Baltimore on April 19, 1861?

   ❑ a. 1st Massachusetts   ❑ b. 3rd Massachusetts
   ❑ c. 6th Massachusetts   ❑ d. 9th Massachusetts

4. What was the monthly pay of a Union private at the end of the war?

   ❑ a. $11   ❑ b. $13
   ❑ c. $16   ❑ d. $18

5. Who led the Union expedition that was defeated at Big Bethel?

   ❑ a. Darius Couch   ❑ b. Benjamin Butler
   ❑ c. James Ricketts   ❑ d. George Meade

6. In which battle was Confederate general James L. Kemper wounded and then captured?

   ❑ a. Antietam   ❑ b. the Wilderness
   ❑ c. Cold Harbor   ❑ d. Gettysburg

7. What was the only Confederate ship to escape the naval battle of Memphis?

   ❑ a. CSS *Colonel Lovell*   ❑ b. CSS *General Earl Van Dorn*
   ❑ c. CSS *Little Rebel*   ❑ d. CSS *General Sterling Price*

8. Which of the following is another name for the battle of Olustee?

   ❑ a. Logan's Crossroads   ❑ b. Rocky Face
   ❑ c. Ocean Pond   ❑ d. Steele's Bayou

9. In which state was Confederate general Leonidas Polk killed by a cannon ball?

   ❑ a. Mississippi   ❑ b. Georgia
   ❑ c. Tennessee   ❑ d. North Carolina

10. What was "Cole" Younger's first name?

   ❑ a. Thomas   ❑ b. James
   ❑ c. John   ❑ d. Robert

> *Georgia has a million of inhabitants. If they can live, we should not starve.*
>
> Willian T. Sherman

QUIZ 63
TRUE OR FALSE

1. Abraham Lincoln caught smallpox during the war.
   ❑ True   ❑ False

2. After the battle of Gettysburg, Robert E. Lee suggested to Jefferson Davis that he be replaced as commander of the Army of Northern Virginia.
   ❑ True   ❑ False

3. The Confederacy never suspended the writ of *habeas corpus*.
   ❑ True   ❑ False

4. More total casualties were suffered during the Seven Days Battles than during the battle of Gettysburg.
   ❑ True   ❑ False

5. No black man won the Medal of Honor for service in the US Navy during the war.
   ❑ True   ❑ False

6. The US Signal Corps never adopted the use of semaphore.
   ❑ True   ❑ False

7. Abraham Lincoln and William T. Sherman first met in 1864.
   ❑ True   ❑ False

8. Despite a Presidential proclamation that Confederate privateers would be hanged as pirates, none were ever executed.
   ❑ True   ❑ False

9. General Joseph Wheeler was never captured by the Union.
   ❑ True   ❑ False

10. General William T. Sherman was one-quarter Native American.
    ❑ True   ❑ False

QUIZ 64
SHORT ANSWER

1. Before the outbreak of the Civil War, which of the following officers had the most seniority in the US Army: Joseph E. Johnston, Robert E. Lee, or Albert Sidney Johnston?

   . . . .

2. Which battle included the ground known as "Hell's Half Acre"?

   . . . .

THE RECRUITING BUSINESS.

VOLUNTEER-BROKER (to Barber) "Look a-here—I want you to trim up this old chap with a flaxen wig and a light mustache, so as to make him look like twenty; and as I shall probably clear three hundred dollars on him, I sha'n't mind giving you fifty for the job."

3. What were *Torch*, *David*, and *Squib*?

   . . . .

4. Who led the Union forces in the battle of Rocky Face Ridge?

   . . . .

5. What was the "Bastille of the Confederacy"?

   . . . .

6. Who was older, Joseph E. Johnston or Jefferson Davis?

   . . . .

7. What were Union troops usually referring to when they
   mentioned the "Tennessee Quickstep"?

   . . . .

8. Did the Loudoun Rangers fight for the Union or Confederacy?

   . . . .

9. Who was the only woman executed for involvement in the
   Lincoln assassination?

   . . . .

10. Which Confederate general was born in Ireland on
    St Patrick's Day?

   . . . .

---

*Do your duty in all things. You cannot do more. You should
never do less.*

Robert E. Lee

QUIZ 65
MULTIPLE CHOICE

1. Who planned and led the Confederate attack on Fort Stedman, the last major offensive of the Army of Northern Virginia?

   ❑ a. John B. Gordon　　❑ b. John Vaughn
   ❑ c. Joseph B. Kershaw　❑ d. Edward Higgins

2. In what current state is the site of the Sand Creek Massacre?

   ❑ a. Oklahoma　　❑ b. Arizona
   ❑ c. Colorado　　❑ d. Idaho

3. Who led the Union forces to victory in the 1863 battle of Droop Mountain?

   ❑ a. John Echols　　❑ b. David Sturgis
   ❑ c. James Hardie　　❑ d. William Averell

4. Which of these battles was NOT fought in Kentucky?

   ❑ a. Kock's Plantation　❑ b. Mill Springs
   ❑ c. Perryville　　　　❑ d. Rowlett's Station

DID YOU KNOW...

On the day he was assassinated, Lincoln pardoned a deserter from the Union Army with a note saying, "I think the boy can do us more good above the ground than underground."

5. Which Confederate general supposedly hid behind a tree instead of leading his men into battle at Stone's River?

   ❑ a. Robert Hoke   ❑ b. Gideon Pillow
   ❑ c. William Scurry   ❑ d. John Gregg

6. Of the following, who was NOT a Confederate corps commander at the battle of Franklin?

   ❑ a. Stephen D. Lee   ❑ b. Edward A. Johnson
   ❑ c. Alexander P. Stewart   ❑ d. Benjamin F. Cheatham

7. On what date was the battle of Iuka fought?

   ❑ a. October 13, 1861   ❑ b. March 22, 1862
   ❑ c. September 19, 1862   ❑ d. November 11, 1862

8. During the war, the Mississippi state flag included which tree?

   ❑ a. sycamore   ❑ b. elm
   ❑ c. oak   ❑ d. magnolia

9. How many stars did a Confederate colonel wear on his collar?

   ❑ a. 0   ❑ b. 1
   ❑ c. 2   ❑ d. 3

10. In what year was the "Missouri Compromise"?

   ❑ a. 1790   ❑ b. 1820
   ❑ c. 1835   ❑ d. 1847

Why do men fight who were born to be brothers?

James Longstreet

QUIZ 66
MATCH UP

Match these battles with the state in which they were fought.

1. Palmetto Ranch

2. Newtonia

3. Pleasant Hill

4. Spring Hill

5. Ringold Gap

6. Brice's Crossroads

7. Rivers' Bridge

8. Day's Gap

9. Mill Springs

10. Monroe's Crossroads

a) Louisiana

b) Georgia

c) Texas

d) Alabama

e) North Carolina

f) Missouri

g) Kentucky

h) Tennessee

i) South Carolina

j) Mississippi

FAMOUS FACES

Name these major Civil War figures.

1.

2.

3.

4.

5.

6.

ANSWERS

QUIZ 37 – MULTIPLE CHOICE
1)b 2)d 3)d 4)a 5)b 6)a 7)a 8)d 9)b 10)c

QUIZ 38 – TRUE OR FALSE
1) True
2) False. He fled after the war but returned in 1869
3) True. He reached the rank of corporal
4) False. The true number is less than 20 percent
5) True. In 1869
6) True
7) False. The idea was discussed in Congress but never approved
8) True
9) False. The CSS *St Patrick* made a failed attack against the USS *Octorara* in 1865
10) False

QUIZ 39 – SHORT ANSWER
1) The North
2) A platoon
3) Before
4) Frederick Douglas
5) Earl Van Dorn
6) Chickamauga and Chattanooga National Military Park
7) "…where the grapes of wrath are stored"
8) The Angel of Marye's Heights
9) The Whig Party
10) A sewing kit

QUIZ 40 – MULTIPLE CHOICE, CIVIL WAR MOVIES
1)b 2)c 3)a 4)d 5)c 6)d 7)d 8)c 9)a 10)c

QUIZ 41 – MATCH UP
1)h 2)a 3)i 4)d 5)f 6)j 7)b 8)g 9)c 10)e

QUIZ 42 – MULTIPLE CHOICE
1)c 2)b 3)b 4)c 5)a 6)d 7)a 8)d 9)c 10)b

QUIZ 43 – TRUE OR FALSE
1) True
2) True
3) False. Mathew Brady photographed the war at his own expense, though he eventually sold his photograph collection to the US government in 1875

4) True

5) True

6) False. Mosby disbanded his command without surrendering

7) True

8) False. He was wounded during Gaines's Mill

9) False. Not even close

10) False. Again, not even close

QUIZ 44 – SHORT ANSWER

1) Six years

2) CSS *Shenandoah*

3) One

4) Wade Hampton

5) A bent or twisted piece of destroyed rail

6) Ambrose Bierce

7) New Orleans

8) .58

9) XXV (25th)

10) The Cumberland

QUIZ 45 – MULTIPLE CHOICE

1)c 2)a 3)b 4)d 5)a 6)c 7)c 8)b 9)a 10)c

QUIZ 46 – MATCH UP

1)i 2)b 3)f 4)h 5)a 6)c 7)j 8)d 9)g 10)e

QUIZ 47 – MULTIPLE CHOICE

1)a 2)b 3)c 4)b 5)d 6)b 7)a 8)c 9)d 10)d

QUIZ 48 – TRUE OR FALSE

1) False. The US Navy employed thousands of African-Americans

2) False

3) True

4) True

5) True. The Army of Northern Virginia had 45

6) False. Fourteen received the medal for actions at New Market Heights alone

7) True

8) True. He married his second wife, Helen Pitts, in 1884

9) True

10) False. He owned one, but freed him. His wife owned several

QUIZ 49 – SHORT ANSWER

1) Harriet Tubman
2) James Longstreet
3) Blue
4) The Monroe Doctrine
5) John Bell Hood and Joseph E. Johnston
6) The Confederacy
7) Austin and Tallahassee
8) The Republic of Texas
9) Antietam
10) The "Whatisit" was the name given to Mathew Brady's portable darkroom by curious Union soldiers

QUIZ 50 – MULTIPLE CHOICE, THE BATTLE OF MOBILE BAY

1)c 2)d 3)a 4)c 5)b 6)a 7)b 8)d 9)b 10)a

QUIZ 51 – MATCH UP

1)j 2)a 3)h 4)e 5)i 6)c 7)g 8)b 9)d 10)f

QUIZ 52 – MULTIPLE CHOICE

1)c 2)b 3)c 4)c 5)a 6)d 7)c 8)a 9)c 10)a

QUIZ 53 – TRUE OR FALSE

1) False. He finished third in his class out of 38
2) True
3) True
4) True
5) False. He died in 1914, several months before the outbreak
6) False. It saw limited use in the Crimean War and the Indian Mutiny
7) True
8) True
9) False
10) False. It began operation before the war

QUIZ 54 – SHORT ANSWER

1) Yes
2) Julia Ward Howe
3) An ordnance sergeant
4) John Ross (Guwisguwi)
5) The Bible
6) Birdseye
7) Morris Island

8) Ohio

9) Colonel Charles Marshall

10) Medical director

QUIZ 55 – MULTIPLE CHOICE
1)b 2)b 3)a 4)c 5)d 6)a 7)b 8)b 9)c 10)a

QUIZ 56 – MATCH UP
1)b 2)i 3)f 4)a 5)g 6)j 7)d 8)c 9)e 10)h

QUIZ 57 – MULTIPLE CHOICE
1)d 2)b 3)d 4)c 5)d 6)a 7)c 8)b 9)a 10)b

QUIZ 58 – TRUE OR FALSE
1) True

2) False. He was dismissed from the Army, but his rank was reinstated in 1882, nearly 20 years before his death

3) False. It never had more than seven at any given time

4) True. He resigned his commission on election day

5) True. Though he referred to himself as a colonel

6) False. They first met on March 8, 1864

7) True

8) True

9) False. Nineteen out of the 22 received the medal

10) True

QUIZ 59 – SHORT ANSWER
1) Six. Andrew Johnson, Ulysses S. Grant, Rutherford B. Hayes, James Garfield, Benjamin Harrison, and William McKinley

2) Captured Confederates who joined the Union Army, usually to fight Indians in the West

3) His right

4) Lewis Addison Armistead

5) Robert E. Lee

6) Alexander H. Stephens

7) Copperheads

8) John Newland Maffitt

9) January 1, 1863

10) After. He was wounded the same day that President Johnson officially declared the war over. He died a few days later

QUIZ 60 – MULTIPLE CHOICE, THE LINCOLN ASSASSINATION
1)b 2)b 3)b 4)c 5)c 6)a 7)d 8)a 9)b 10)b

QUIZ 61 – MATCH UP
1)g 2)d 3)c 4)j 5)f 6)a 7)e 8)i 9)b 10)h

QUIZ 62 – MULTIPLE CHOICE
1)c 2)a 3)c 4)c 5)b 6)d 7)b 8)c 9)b 10)a

QUIZ 63 – TRUE OR FALSE
1) True. Fortunately for him, it was a mild case of the virus
2) True
3) False
4) False
5) False
6) True. They used wig-wag signaling
7) False. They'd met once in the early days of the war
8) True
9) False. He was captured while fleeing to Mexico
10) False

QUIZ 64 – SHORT ANSWER
1) Joseph E. Johnston
2) Murfreesboro (or Stone's River)
3) Confederate torpedo boats
4) William T. Sherman
5) Libby Prison in Richmond
6) Joseph E. Johnston, by a year
7) Diarrhea
8) The Union
9) Mary Elizabeth Jenkins Surratt
10) Patrick Cleburne

QUIZ 65 – MULTIPLE CHOICE
1)a 2)c 3)d 4)a 5)b 6)b 7)c 8)d 9)d 10)b

QUIZ 66 – MATCH UP
1)c 2)f 3)a 4)h 5)b 6)j 7)i 8)d 9)g 10)e

QUIZ 67 – FAMOUS FACES
1) Gordon Granger, Union general
2) Sterling Price, Confederate general
3) Benjamin Grierson, Union cavalry general
4) Jefferson C. Davis, Union general
5) John C. Pemberton, Confederate general
6) David D. Porter, Union admiral

DIFFICULT
QUESTIONS

THREE-STAR
GENERAL
KNOWLEDGE

QUIZ 68
MULTIPLE CHOICE

1. Which Union ship captured the CSS *Florida*?

   ❏ a. USS *Wachusett*   ❏ b. USS *Kearsarge*
   ❏ c. USS *Malvern*   ❏ d. USS *Weehawken*

2. Horace Greeley was editor of which newspaper?

   ❏ a. *New York Herald*   ❏ b. *New York Times*
   ❏ c. *New York Tribune* ❏ d. *Harper's Weekly Journal of Civilization*

3. In which year was Confederate cavalry general Turner Ashby killed?

   ❏ a. 1861   ❏ b. 1862
   ❏ c. 1863   ❏ d. 1864

4. Which battle is sometimes known as "Kilpatrick's Shirttail Skedaddle"?

   ❏ a. White Hall   ❏ b. Monroe's Crossroads
   ❏ c. Kinston   ❏ d. Goldsboro Bridge

5. According to regulations, how many buttons did a Confederate general have on his coat?

   ❏ a. 8   ❏ b. 12
   ❏ c. 16   ❏ d. 20

6. Of the following, who was NOT a corps commander at the battle of Shiloh?

   ❑ a. Leonidas Polk   ❑ b. Braxton Bragg
   ❑ c. P.G.T. Beauregard   ❑ d. William Hardee

7. On which battlefield would you find Spangler's Spring?

   ❑ a. Gettysburg   ❑ b. Antietam
   ❑ c. Seven Pines   ❑ d. Five Forks

8. In 1862, which Union general was relieved of his command after refusing to disband a regiment of black soldiers he had raised without orders?

   ❑ a. Benjamin Butler   ❑ b. Nathaniel P. Banks
   ❑ c. David Hunter   ❑ d. John C. Frémont

9. The Spencer carbine carried how many shots in its magazine?

   ❑ a. 5   ❑ b. 6
   ❑ c. 7   ❑ d. 8

10. On which battlefield can you see the "Eternal Light Peace Memorial"?

   ❑ a. Antietam   ❑ b. Manassas
   ❑ c. Appomattox   ❑ d. Gettysburg

You are better off than I am, for while you have lost your left, I have lost my right arm.

Robert E. Lee to Thomas J. "Stonewall" Jackson

QUIZ 69
TRUE OR FALSE

1. Union general Charles Edward Phelps invented the percussion cap in 1832.
   ❏ True   ❏ False

2. Union Medal of Honor winner Arthur MacArthur was the father of US World War II general Douglas MacArthur.
   ❏ True   ❏ False

3. J.E.B. Stuart suffered no casualties to his command during its 1862 ride around McClellan's army.
   ❏ True   ❏ False

4. The Confederacy never repealed the law that allowed men to avoid the draft by hiring a replacement or paying a fee.
   ❏ True   ❏ False

5. Both the Union and the Confederacy had ships named *Florida*.
   ❏ True   ❏ False

6. The Confederate Constitution prohibited a revival of the slave trade.
   ❏ True   ❏ False

7. William T. Sherman suffered from asthma.
   ❏ True   ❏ False

8. Only a dozen ironclads were ever commissioned into Confederate service.
   ❏ True   ❏ False

9. At the outbreak of the war, the population of New Orleans was greater than Richmond and Atlanta put together.
   ❏ True   ❏ False

10. Before the war, John C. Frémont resigned from the US Army after being found guilty of mutiny.

❏ True   ❏ False

© Simon Tofield

QUIZ 70
SHORT ANSWER

1. In the Confederate Army, who was paid more, a surgeon or a chaplain?

   ....

2. Where in the United States was slavery first officially abolished?

   ....

3. Confederate general Edward "Allegheny" Johnson was captured during which battle?

   ....

4. What previously independent US Army Corps was amalgamated into the Corps of Engineers in 1863?

   ....

5. Who was assigned the task of rebuilding and reorganizing the US Army Artillery after First Bull Run?

   ....

DID YOU KNOW...

In 1958, the United States passed a law which enabled the last two surviving Confederate veterans to draw Federal pensions.

6. What did the letters "AD" and "BC" mean when worn on a Union cap?

....

7. Which Union general was captured by John S. Mosby in his famous "Fairfax Courthouse Raid"?

....

8. What was the highest-numbered Florida volunteer regiment to serve during the war?

....

9. What was a *vivandiére*?

....

10. Who was the US Army's first "signal officer"?

....

June 3. Cold Harbor. I was killed.

The last diary entry of a Union soldier killed at Cold Harbor

QUIZ 71

MULTIPLE CHOICE, RAPHAEL SEMMES AND THE CSS *ALABAMA*

1. How many ships did Raphael Semmes capture, destroy or ransom during the war?

   ☐ a. 63   ☐ b. 67
   ☐ c. 74   ☐ d. 83

2. In which state was Raphael Semmes born?

   ☐ a. Maryland   ☐ b. North Carolina
   ☐ c. Delaware   ☐ d. New Jersey

3. How many guns did the CSS *Alabama* carry into battle with the USS *Kearsarge*?

   ☐ a. 4   ☐ b. 6
   ☐ c. 8   ☐ d. 12

4. On what day of the week did the CSS *Alabama* and the USS *Kearsarge* fight their duel?

   ☐ a. Monday   ☐ b. Wednesday
   ☐ c. Friday   ☐ d. Sunday

5. Who was the executive officer on the CSS *Alabama*?

   ☐ a. Richard Armstrong   ☐ b. John Kell
   ☐ c. John Low   ☐ d. Arthur Sinclair

6. What was the name of the British yacht that rescued Raphael Semmes from the water after he abandoned the CSS *Alabama*?

☐ a. *Messenger*   ☐ b. *Daisy*
☐ c. *Deerhound*   ☐ d. *Swan*

7. While under construction, what numerical designation was assigned to the ship that would become the CSS *Alabama*?

☐ a. 90   ☐ b. 180
☐ c. 290   ☐ d. 360

8. What was the first prize taken by the CSS *Alabama*?

☐ a. *Starlight*   ☐ b. *Ocmulgee*

☐ c. *Ocean Rover*   ☐ d. *Alert*

9. Raphael Semmes surrendered as part of the command of which general?

☐ a. Robert E. Lee   ☐ b. Joseph E. Johnston

☐ c. Edmund Kirby Smith   ☐ d. Richard Taylor

10. Which ship did Raphael Semmes command during the Mexican–American War?

☐ a. USS *Sprite*   ☐ b. USS *Somers*

☐ c. USS *Flitter*   ☐ d. USS *Doner*

ANAGRAMS

"Truest Form"

(Answers on page 216)

MATCH UP

Match these battles with another name for the same battle.

1. Front Royal

a) Guard Hill

2. Chickasaw Bayou

b) Deep Run

3. First Deep Bottom Run

c) Pleasant Grove

4. Franklin's Crossing

d) King's School House

5. Glendale

e) Walnut Hills

6. Mansfield

f) Peeble's Farm

7. Haw's Shop

g) Bloody Bridge

8. Waterloo Plantation

h) Fryer's Farm

9. Oak Grove

i) Enon Church

10. Poplar Springs Church

j) Strawberry Plains

DIFFICULT

QUIZ 73
MULTIPLE CHOICE

1. In what state is the National Museum of Civil War Medicine?

    ☐ a. Virginia   ☐ b. Maryland
    ☐ c. Pennsylvania   ☐ d. West Virginia

2. Who led the Union forces at the battle of La Glorietta Pass?

    ☐ a. John Slough   ☐ b. Sterling Price
    ☐ c. David Twiggs   ☐ d. James H. Carelton

3. Who was the commandant of the US Marine Corps at the outbreak of the war?

    ☐ a. John Harris   ☐ b. Jacob Zeilen
    ☐ c. Allyn Stillman   ☐ d. John Wilson Haverstick

THE DANGEROUS PLAYMATE—A SINGULAR INSTANCE OF FASCINATION.
That Innocent Infant JOHNY BULL giving Aid and Comfort to the Reptile.

4. The giant Parrott rifle known as "Swamp Angel" exploded while shelling which city?

   ☐ a. Richmond   ☐ b. Vicksburg
   ☐ c. Charleston   ☐ d. Petersburg

5. In the 1862 agreement on the exchange of prisoners, a general officer was equal to how many enlisted men?

   ☐ a. 1   ☐ b. 20
   ☐ c. 50   ☐ d. 60

6. Which of the following ships was NEVER commanded by John Newland Maffitt?

   ☐ a. CSS *Florida*   ☐ b. CSS *Albemarle*
   ☐ c. CSS *Bat*   ☐ d. CSS *Owl*

7. Which of these Charleston defenses was farthest north?

   ☐ a. Battery Wagner   ☐ b. Fort Sumter
   ☐ c. Fort Johnson   ☐ d. Fort Moutrie

8. Confederate general Paul Jones Semmes was mortally wounded during which battle?

   ☐ a. Fredericksburg   ☐ b. Chancellorsville
   ☐ c. Gettysburg   ☐ d. Spotsylvania Courthouse

9. Whose division led the Union attack into the Petersburg crater?

   ☐ a. James H. Ledlie   ☐ b. Orlando Wilcox
   ☐ c. Edward Ferro   ☐ d. John Potter

10. Approximately how many dollars did John S. Mosby and his men ride off with during the "Greenback Raid"?

    ☐ a. $12,000   ☐ b. $87,000
    ☐ c. $102,000   ☐ d. $173,000

TRUE OR FALSE

1. The Union Army suffered no casualties while inflicting nearly 600 in their clash with Georgia militia at the battle of Griswoldville.

   ❑ True   ❑ False

2. By 1865, the Union employed black men in every branch of the Army.

   ❑ True   ❑ False

3. The Federate Military Telegraph System was turned over to the US Army in 1863.

   ❑ True   ❑ False

4. Fourteen Confederate generals became casualties at the battle of Franklin.

   ❑ True   ❑ False

5. President Lincoln invited General Grant to come to Ford's Theater with him on the night he was killed.

   ❑ True   ❑ False

6. By 1860, the United States was the only country left in the Western Hemisphere where slavery was still legal.

   ❑ True   ❑ False

Once let the black man get upon his person the brass letters U.S.; let him get an eagle on his button, and a musket on his shoulder, and bullets in his pocket, and there is no power on earth or under the earth which can deny that he has earned the right of citizenship in the United States.

Frederick Douglas

7. After serving out his term as President, Andrew Johnson was later elected to and served in the US Senate.

    ❑ True   ❑ False

8. In the 1862 battle of Mill Springs in Kentucky, the Union Army charged *northward* across the battlefield.

    ❑ True   ❑ False

9. There are over 100 documented cases of women disguised as men fighting in the Civil War.

    ❑ True   ❑ False

10. William J. Hardee was captured during the Mexican-American War.

    ❑ True   ❑ False

THE FINANCES OF THE REBELLION.

QUIZ 75
SHORT ANSWER

1. Did Americans practice April Fools' Day during the war?

   . . . .

2. By what other name was the giant Union railroad mortar "Dictator" known?

   . . . .

3. Who was the Assistant Secretary of the Navy of the United States during the war?

   . . . .

4. Which Union general was sometimes called "The Russian Thunderbolt"?

   . . . .

5. Who surrendered the last body of uniformed Confederate troops east of the Mississippi?

   . . . .

6. What was the official name of Andersonville Prison?

   . . . .

DID YOU KNOW...

Abraham Lincoln's oldest son Robert Todd Lincoln would eventually serve as US Secretary of War under Presidents Chester Arthur and James Garfield.

7. Which two former Presidents of the United States died in 1862?

. . . .

8. Who killed General Earl Van Dorn?

. . . .

9. Which was a higher rank in the Union Navy: vice admiral or rear admiral?

. . . .

10. Which future Union general fought at the battles of Solferino and Magenta despite having only one arm – having lost the other in the Mexican-American War?

. . . .

ANAGRAMS

"Try Sunglasses"

(Answers on page 216)

QUIZ 76
MULTIPLE CHOICE

1. Approximately how many Medals of Honor were awarded during the Civil War?

   ❏ a. 600   ❏ b. 900
   ❏ c. 1,500   ❏ d. 2,300

2. How many men accompanied John Brown on his famous raid?

   ❏ a. 9   ❏ b. 13
   ❏ c. 17   ❏ d. 21

3. Which one of these engagements during the Petersburg campaign occurred first?

   ❏ a. Jerusalem Plank Road   ❏ b. the Crater
   ❏ c. Globe Tavern   ❏ d. Reams Station

4. In 1862, where did Union gunboats exchange "iron valentines" with the Confederates?

   ❏ a. Fort Henry   ❏ b. Fort Donelson
   ❏ c. Island No. 10   ❏ d. Vicksburg

5. In which state is the Carnifex Ferry battlefield located?

   ❏ a. Virginia   ❏ b. West Virginia
   ❏ c. Tennessee   ❏ d. North Carolina

6. Which battle is sometimes called "Florida's Alamo"?

   ❏ a. Natural Bridge   ❏ b. Olustee
   ❏ c. Marianna   ❏ d. Campbellton

7. Which of these battles was NOT fought in Missouri?

☐ a. Little Blue River ☐ b. Roan's Tan Yard
☐ c. Cabin Creek ☐ d. Dry Wood Creek

8. George Sholter James, the man who fired the "first shot" on Fort Sumter, was later mortally wounded during which battle?

☐ a. South Mountain ☐ b. Cedar Mountain
☐ c. Kennesaw Mountain ☐ d. Cedar Creek

9. How many shots did a Kerr Patent Revolver hold in its cylinder?

☐ a. 4 ☐ b. 5
☐ c. 6 ☐ d. 7

10. Confederate general William R. Scurry was mortally wounded during which battle?

☐ a. Mansfield ☐ b. Pleasant River
☐ c. Jenkins' Ferry ☐ d. Valverde

VOLUNTEERING DOWN DIXIE.

MATCH UP

Match these Union generals with their West Point class ranking.

1. Ulysses S. Grant

   a) 2nd in 1846

2. William Rosencrans

   b) 32nd in 1841

3. John M. Schofield

   c) 3rd in 1839

4. William Franklin Buell

   d) 21st in 1843

5. Henry Halleck

   e) 18th in 1847

6. George B. McClellan

   f) 6th in 1840

7. William T. Sherman

   g) 1st in 1843

8. Ambrose Burnside

   h) Did not attend West Point

9. Winfield Scott

   i) 7th in 1853

10. Don Carlos Buell

    j) 5th in 1842

MULTIPLE CHOICE

1. Abraham Lincoln removed Secretary of War Simon Cameron by sending him as ambassador to which country?

   ❑ a. France   ❑ b. Brazil
   ❑ c. Russia   ❑ d. Turkey

2. Oliver Otis Howard lost his arm during which battle?

   ❑ a. Fair Oaks   ❑ b. First Manassas
   ❑ c. Antietam   ❑ d. Second Manassas

3. The 1864 Democratic Convention was held in which city?

   ❑ a. New York   ❑ b. Baltimore
   ❑ c. Chicago   ❑ d. Philadelphia

4. Who captained the ironclad CSS *Savannah* for the majority of her service life?

   ❑ a. William F. Hunter   ❑ b. Robert F. Pinkney
   ❑ c. John Newland Maffitt ❑ d. Josiah Tatnall

5. The standard US Cavalry saddle shared its name with which general?

   ❑ a. Burnside   ❑ b. Hooker
   ❑ c. Sherman   ❑ d. McClellan

6. In which year was the battle of High Bridge fought?

   ❑ a. 1862   ❑ b. 1863
   ❑ c. 1864   ❑ d. 1865

7. Of the eight military institutions in the United States at the outbreak of the war, how many were located in southern states?

    ❑ a. 0   ❑ b. 3
    ❑ c. 7   ❑ d. 8

8. In which state is Castle Pinckney located?

    ❑ a. Virginia   ❑ b. Georgia
    ❑ c. North Carolina   ❑ d. South Carolina

9. Which battle witnessed the assault on Henry House Hill?

    ❑ a. First Manassas   ❑ b. Chickamauga
    ❑ c. Perryville   ❑ d. Mechanicsville

10. Who was the Chief Engineer of the Army of the Potomac at the battle of Gettysburg?

    ❑ a. Sumner Carruth   ❑ b. Gouverneur K. Warren
    ❑ c. Manning F. Force   ❑ d. Lewis B. Parsons

THE GUNBOAT CANDIDATE
AT THE BATTLE OF MALVERN HILL.

TRUE OR FALSE

1. Andrew Johnson was born the year before Abraham Lincoln.
   ❑ True   ❑ False

2. During the war, two British Royal Navy officers were captured while serving as Confederate blockade-runners.
   ❑ True   ❑ False

3. The Civil War saw the first use of railroads to move troops during wartime.
   ❑ True   ❑ False

4. Confederate general Stand Watie had marched on the "Trail of Tears."
   ❑ True   ❑ False

5. More than 50 percent of Civil War soldiers buried in National Cemeteries are unidentified.
   ❑ True   ❑ False

6. Allan Pinkerton refused to continue to gather intelligence for the Union Army after McClellan's removal from command in September of 1862.
   ❑ True   ❑ False

DIFFICULT

> *General, I have been a soldier all my life. I have been with soldiers, engaged in fights by couples, squads, companies, regiments, divisions and armies, and should know as well as anyone what soldiers can do. It is my opinion that no 15,000 men ever arrayed for battle can take that position.*
>
> James Longstreet to Robert E. Lee at Gettysburg

7. After the war, John Schofield served as Secretary of War, Superintendent of West Point, and General-in-Chief of the US Army.

   ❑ True   ❑ False

8. The 54th Massachusetts was the first colored regiment raised in the North.

   ❑ True   ❑ False

9. The Army Medal of Honor was the first medal that could be worn openly in the American military.

   ❑ True   ❑ False

10. The Civil War Preservation Trust has now saved over 30,000 acres of Civil War battlefields.

    ❑ True   ❑ False

On they come with the old swinging route step and swaying battle flags. Before us in proud humiliation stood the embodiment of manhood. Thin, worn and famished, but erect and with eyes looking level into ours. Waking memories that bound us together as no other bond. Was not such manhood to be welcomed back into the Union so tested and assured. On our part not a sound of trumpet more nor roll of drum, not a cheer, nor word, nor whisper of vain glorying, nor motion of man. But an awed stillness rather and breathholding, as if it were the passing of the dead.

Joshua Chamberlain on the surrender of the Army of Northern Virginia

SHORT ANSWER

1. Which was the bigger killer of soldiers during the war, typhoid or dysentery?

....

D. Murphy's Son, Print, 65 Fulton & 372 Pearl Street, N. Y.

Poor deluded Miss-Souri takes a Secession bath, and finds it much hotter than she expected !

2. Did General Orlando M. Poe serve the Confederacy or the Union?

. . . .

3. Who led the Confederate boarding party that captured and then burned the USS *Underwriter*?

. . . .

4. Who was head of the Mexican government in 1861?

. . . .

5. Who was the only Union general mortally wounded during the battle of Chickamauga?

. . . .

6. The Confederate Naval School was housed in which ship?

. . . .

7. Along with chalk and honey, what was the main ingredient of "calomel," one of the most commonly prescribed curatives in both armies?

. . . .

8. Which letter of the alphabet did the Union purposely avoid using to identify the company of a regiment?

. . . .

9. Which Union general wrote *Ben-Hur*?

. . . .

10. Which President officially reinstated Robert E. Lee as a United States citizen?

. . . .

QUIZ 81

MULTIPLE CHOICE, JOSHUA CHAMBERLAIN AND THE 20TH MAINE

DIFFICULT

1. Who was the first colonel of the 20th Maine regiment?

   ❑ a. Joshua Chamberlain ❑ b. Ellis Spear
   ❑ c. Adelbert Ames   ❑ d. William Bickford

2. Where did the 20th Maine first come under enemy fire?

   ❑ a. Shepherdstown Ford ❑ b. Fredericksburg
   ❑ c. Chancellorsville   ❑ d. Middleburg

3. From which college did Joshua Chamberlain receive his education?

   ❑ a. Bangor University   ❑ b. University of Cambridge
   ❑ c. Massachusetts Institute ❑ d. Bowdoin College
      of Technology

4. Which disease caused the 20th Maine to be temporarily sidelined after the battle of Fredericksburg?

   ❑ a. cholera   ❑ b. dysentery
   ❑ c. smallpox ❑ d. bubonic plague

5. Before the battle of Gettysburg, the 20th Maine received a group of "mutineers" who were sent over from which disbanded Maine regiment?

   ❑ a. 1st ❑ b. 2nd
   ❑ c. 6th ❑ d. 9th

6. Who commanded the brigade that included the 20th Maine at the beginning of the battle of Gettysburg?

    ❏ a. Adelbert Ames   ❏ b. Strong Vincent
    ❏ c. James Rice   ❏ d. Charles Phelps

7. How many times was Joshua Chamberlain hit by small-arms fire during the defense of Little Round Top?

    ❏ a. 0   ❏ b. 2
    ❏ c. 4   ❏ d. 5

8. The 20th Maine spent most of the war as part of which corps in the Army of the Potomac?

    ❏ a. 5th   ❏ b. 10th
    ❏ c. 15th   ❏ d. 20th

9. How many terms did Joshua Chamberlain serve as Governor of Maine?

    ❏ a. 1   ❏ b. 2
    ❏ c. 3   ❏ d. 4

10. Which of these works was NOT written by Joshua Chamberlain?

    ❏ a. *A Soldier's Life*   ❏ b. *In the Hands of Providence*
    ❏ c. *The Passing of Armies*   ❏ d. *My Story of Fredericksburg*

I think that Lee should have been hanged. It was all the worse that he was a good man and a fine character and acted conscientiously. It's always the good men who do the most harm in the world.

Henry Adams

MATCH UP

Match these Confederate commanders with their West Point class ranking.

1. A.P. Hill

a) 15th in 1847

2. Thomas J. "Stonewall" Jackson

b) 13th in 1840

3. James Longstreet

c) 54th in 1842

4. P. G. T. Beauregard

d) 8th in 1826

5. Jubal Early

e) 5th in 1837

6. Robert E. Lee

f) 2nd in 1829

7. Braxton Bragg

g) 2nd in 1838

8. Richard Ewell

h) 17th in 1846

9. Joseph E. Johnston

i) 13th in 1829

10. Albert Sidney Johnston

j) 18th in 1837

MULTIPLE CHOICE

1. From which state did the "Fire Zouaves" originate?

   ☐ a. New York   ☐ b. Pennsylvania
   ☐ c. Ohio   ☐ d. Maine

THE FOOD QUESTION DOWN SOUTH.

JEFF DAVIS. "See! see! the beautiful Boots just come to me from the dear ladies of Baltimore!"

BEAUREGARD. "Ha! Boots? Boots? When shall we eat them? Now?"

2. Which of these Union ironclads was sunk by a torpedo in 1863?

  ❑ a. USS *Baron De Kalb*   ❑ b. USS *Benton*
  ❑ c. USS *Pittsburg*   ❑ d. USS *Chillicothe*

3. In total, how many men were awarded the rank of general by the Congress of the Confederate States of America?

  ❑ a. 338   ❑ b. 425
  ❑ c. 499   ❑ d. 536

4. The Confederate cannon "Whistling Dick" helped defend which city?

  ❑ a. Charleston   ❑ b. Vicksburg
  ❑ c. New Orleans   ❑ d. Atlanta

5. What is generally considered the "westernmost" battle of the Civil War?

  ❑ a. La Glorietta Pass   ❑ b. Sabine Crossroads
  ❑ c. Picacho Peak   ❑ d. Pea Ridge

6. Who was the founder and first President of the Southern Historical Society?

  ❑ a. Braxton Bragg   ❑ b. George Norton
  ❑ c. Edward P. Alexander ❑ d. Dabney Maury

The hair to be short: the beard to be worn at the pleasure of the individual; but, when worn, to be kept short and neatly trimmed.

Regulations for the Army of the Confederate States, 1861

7. Approximately how much did the barrel of a standard mountain howitzer weigh?

   ❑ a. 100lb ❑ b. 220lb
   ❑ c. 360lb ❑ d. 530lb

8. How many men served as Secretary of War for the Confederacy?

   ❑ a. 3 ❑ b. 4
   ❑ c. 5 ❑ d. 6

9. Which Confederate ironclad sank the USS *Southfield* in 1864?

   ❑ a. CSS *Atlanta* ❑ b. CSS *Nashville*
   ❑ c. CSS *Virginia II* ❑ d. CSS *Albemarle*

10. Which Union general was killed in 1873 during negotiations with Modoc Indians?

   ❑ a. Samuel Ryan Curtis ❑ b. Hugh Judson Kilpatrick
   ❑ c. Edward R.S. Canby ❑ d. John Alexander Logan

ANAGRAMS

"Panda On Canal"

(Answers on page 216)

QUIZ 84
TRUE OR FALSE

1. The Emancipation Proclamation freed no slaves on the day it came into effect.
   ❑ True   ❑ False

2. The Confederacy passed the first conscription law in American history.
   ❑ True   ❑ False

3. The 6th Pennsylvania Cavalry, also known as "Rush's Lancers" were never armed with lances.
   ❑ True   ❑ False

4. The Williams Rapid-Fire Gun was never used in combat.
   ❑ True   ❑ False

5. Abraham Lincoln was once part-owner of a tavern.
   ❑ True   ❑ False

6. John C. Frémont was on the presidential ballot in 1864.
   ❑ True   ❑ False

7. Union general Oliver Otis Howard went on to help found Howard University.
   ❑ True   ❑ False

8. Prince Albert, husband of Queen Victoria, died during the war.
   ❑ True   ❑ False

9. There are no verifiable accounts of a Union unit breaking due solely to hearing the "rebel yell."
   ❑ True   ❑ False

10. The Internal Revenue Service was established during the war.
    ❑ True   ❑ False

SHORT ANSWER

1. What organization changed its name to the "Sons of Liberty" in 1865?

   ....

2. To whom did Ulysses S. Grant assign the task of delivering his first message to Robert E. Lee, suggesting the surrender of the Army of Northern Virginia after the fall of Richmond?

   ....

3. Where did Raphael Semmes abandon the CSS *Sumter*?

   ....

4. What were the last two words of John Wilkes Booth?

   ....

5. In the Union Army, how many bars did a second lieutenant wear on his shoulders?

   ....

6. Who did Major-General Joseph Hooker appoint to create and lead the Bureau of Military Information in 1863?

   ....

7. Who was the last Confederate general to officially surrender?

   ....

8. Which is heavier, a US Springfield Model 1861 or the British Enfield Pattern 1853?

   ....

9. Who carried a red flag with a white square in the center?

. . . .

10. Which was heavier, a Sharps rifle or a Spencer rifle?

. . . .

LITTLE MAC'S UNION SQUEEZE.

MULTIPLE CHOICE

1. William Howard Russell famously wrote for which newspaper during the war?

    ❏ a. *Harper's Weekly*   ❏ b. *New York Times*
    ❏ c. *Baltimore Sun*   ❏ d. *The Times* of London

2. Which of these Union generals was born and died in what is now Germany?

    ❏ a. Peter Joseph Osterhaus   ❏ b. Edward Otho Cresap Ord
    ❏ c. John Alexander Logan   ❏ d. Alpheus Starkey Williams

3. Out of all the battlefield casualties in the war, approximately what percentage were listed as "dead"?

    ❏ a. 10 percent   ❏ b. 20 percent
    ❏ c. 30 percent   ❏ d. 35 percent

4. Who surrendered the Union garrison at Harpers Ferry to "Stonewall" Jackson in 1862?

    ❏ a. George W. Scott   ❏ b. James Shackelford
    ❏ c. Dixon S. Miles   ❏ d. Thomas Ewing

> *The lives of our soldiers are too precious to be sacrificed in the attainment of successes that inflict no loss upon the enemy beyond the actual loss in battle.*
>
> Robert E. Lee

5. Who was the first commander of the United Confederate Veterans?

 ❑ a. John B. Gordon ❑ b. John Vaughn
 ❑ c. Joseph B. Kershaw ❑ d. Edward Higgins

6. How many stars were on the first national flag of the Confederacy?

 ❑ a. 7 ❑ b. 9
 ❑ c. 11 ❑ d. 13

7. The first amphibious landing of the war saw Union forces capture which fort?

 ❑ a. Kitty Hawk ❑ b. Ocracoke
 ❑ c. Hatteras ❑ d. Roanoke

8. Who wrote the poem *Sheridan's Ride*?

 ❑ a. Charles Dawson Shanly ❑ b. Oliver Wendell Holmes
 ❑ c. Walt Whitman ❑ d. Thomas Buchanan Reed

9. Private Peter Pelican of the 36th Illinois is sometimes credited with firing the shot that killed which Confederate general?

 ❑ a. A.P. Hill ❑ b. J.E.B. Stuart
 ❑ c. Ben McCulloch ❑ d. Albert Sidney Johnston

10. Who led the "Indian Brigade" at the battle of Pea Ridge?

 ❑ a. Albert Pike ❑ b. James McIntosh
 ❑ c. Louis Hebert ❑ d. Stand Watie

MATCH UP

Match up these Union corps with their badge symbol.

1. I Corps

2. II Corps

3. III Corps

4. IV Corps

5. V Corps

6. VIII Corps

7. XV Corps

8. XVII Corps

9. XXIII Corps

10. XXIV Corps

a) triangle

b) three-leaf clover

c) cartridge box with the number "40"

d) arrow

e) heart

f) Maltese cross

g) circle

h) diamond

i) shield

j) six-pointed star

MULTIPLE CHOICE

1. What color was the regulation sash for surgeons in the Confederate Army?

   ❏ a. blue   ❏ b. red
   ❏ c. gold   ❏ d. green

2. In which state was the battle of Fort De Russy?

   ❏ a. Virginia   ❏ b. Alabama
   ❏ c. Louisiana   ❏ d. North Carolina

3. Which regiment was NOT an original member of the "Iron Brigade"?

   ❏ a. 19th Indiana   ❏ b. 6th Wisconsin
   ❏ c. 7th Wisconsin   ❏ d. 24th Michigan

4. Who was the first commander of the Confederate Army of Mobile?

   ❏ a. Jones Withers   ❏ b. James Terrill
   ❏ c. John Preston   ❏ d. Alexander Reynolds

5. During which month in 1865 did Union troops capture Richmond?

   ❏ a. March   ❏ b. April
   ❏ c. May   ❏ d. June

DIFFICULT

6. The Confederate ironclad ram CSS *Stonewall* was constructed in which country?

   ❑ a. Britain   ❑ b. France
   ❑ c. Denmark   ❑ d. the Netherlands

7. Who was the first US Army officer to receive the thanks of Congress during the war?

   ❑ a. William Rosencrans   ❑ b. Nathaniel Banks
   ❑ c. Nathaniel Lyon   ❑ d. Ambrose Burnside

8. The commerce raider CSS *Sumter* was later used as a blockade runner under what name?

   ❑ a. *Owl*   ❑ b. *Gibraltar*
   ❑ c. *Lillian*   ❑ d. *Hansa*

9. Who commanded the Irish Brigade during the 1862 battle of Antietam?

   ❑ a. Thomas Meagher   ❑ b. Patrick Kelly
   ❑ c. Daniel Sickles   ❑ d. Thomas Cobb

10. Which future Confederate general wrote *Rifles and Rifle Practice*?

   ❑ a. D.H. Hill
   ❑ b. Sterling Price
   ❑ c. Benjamin F. Cheatham
   ❑ d. Cadmus Marcellus Wilcox

If I owned Texas and Hell, I'd rent out Texas and live in Hell.

General Philip H. Sheridan

TRUE OR FALSE

1. During the war, the US Army allowed Jews to serve as chaplains.
   ❏ True   ❏ False

2. By the time Richmond fell, the war was costing the US government over $2 million a day.
   ❏ True   ❏ False

3. General Robert E. Lee eventually relieved Pickett of his command.
   ❏ True   ❏ False

4. In the first two years of the war, the Confederate government banned the export of cotton.
   ❏ True   ❏ False

THE CHAS-ED "OLD LADY" OF THE C.S.A.

5. The US government allowed soldiers to send letters for free in the later part of the war.
   ❑ True   ❑ False

6. It is currently legal to carry a firearm on the Gettysburg battlefield.
   ❑ True   ❑ False

7. Over 10 percent of all Confederate soldiers were killed or mortally wounded in battle.
   ❑ True   ❑ False

8. The Union Army forced the Confederates to retreat from the field in the 1862 battle of Lone Jack in Missouri.
   ❑ True   ❑ False

9. The Confederate Congress passed the Negro Soldier Bill in March 1865.
   ❑ True   ❑ False

10. James Longstreet's second wife died in 1979.
   ❑ True   ❑ False

DID YOU KNOW...

In 1862 the United States and the Confederacy agreed that medical officers be treated as noncombatants. Although the agreement was haphazardly applied, most captured surgeons were allowed to tend their wounded without interference by opposing forces and, if captured, were immediately released.

SHORT ANSWER

1. Who was the first chairman of the Joint Congressional Committee on the Conduct of the War?

....

© Simon Tofield

2. Which Confederate general authored *Consideration of the Sermon on the Mount* and *The Crucifixion of Christ* in the years before the war?

. . . .

3. Union general Prince Felix Salm-Salm was a native of what country?

. . . .

4. Who was the last surviving man to have held a lieutenant-general commission in the Confederate Army?

. . . .

5. Which US Navy ship was the focus of the "Seward-Meigs-Porter Affair"?

. . . .

6. Who was the Confederate Navy Chief of (Naval) Ordnance and Hydrography, who previously designed and built the ordnance and armor of the CSS *Virginia*?

. . . .

7. Who was the only woman to be awarded the Medal of Honor?

. . . .

8. Regiments from which state had the highest desertion rate in the Confederate forces?

. . . .

9. How many European-built ironclads served in the navy of the Confederacy?

. . . .

10. Who killed Union general William Nelson?

. . . .

MULTIPLE CHOICE, THOMAS FRANCIS MEAGHER AND THE IRISH BRIGADE

1. Thomas Francis Meagher, founder of the Irish Brigade, escaped from which island in 1852 to reach America?

   - ❏ a. the Isle of Man
   - ❏ b. South Island, New Zealand
   - ❏ c. Jamaica
   - ❏ d. Tasmania

2. The Irish Brigade fought in which corps of the Army of the Potomac?

   - ❏ a. I
   - ❏ b. II
   - ❏ c. III
   - ❏ d. IV

3. Which of these regiments was NOT a part of the Irish Brigade?

   - ❏ a. 12th New York
   - ❏ b. 69th New York
   - ❏ c. 116th Pennsylvania
   - ❏ d. 29th Massachusetts

4. Who was mortally wounded leading the Irish Brigade at Cold Harbor?

   - ❏ a. Thomas Meagher
   - ❏ b. Richard Byrne
   - ❏ c. Patrick Kelly
   - ❏ d. Robert Nugent

5. What color was the four-leaf clover worn on the caps of the Irish Brigade?

   - ❏ a. green
   - ❏ b. gold
   - ❏ c. silver
   - ❏ d. red

DIFFICULT

6. Thomas Meagher served as the governor of which state after the war?

❑ a. New York ❑ b. Massachusetts
❑ c. Montana ❑ d. Wyoming

7. What was the last regiment to be incorporated into the brigade?

❑ a. 12th New York ❑ b. 29th Massachusetts
❑ c. 116th Pennsylvania ❑ d. 7th New York Heavy Artillery

8. Which commander of the brigade was killed at Petersburg?

❑ a. Richard Byrnes ❑ b. Thomas Smyth
❑ c. Patrick Kelly ❑ d. Robert Nugent

9. What is the meaning of "*Faugh-a-Ballagh*," the nickname of the 28th Massachusetts?

❑ a. March to Victory ❑ b. Freedom in Death
❑ c. Clear the Way ❑ d. Always Forward

10. How did Thomas Meagher eventually die?

❑ a. shot in the back ❑ b. drowned
❑ c. poisoned ❑ d. kicked by a horse

My plans are perfect, and when I start to carry them out, may God have mercy on Bobby Lee, for I shall have none.

"Fighting" Joe Hooker

QUIZ 92
MATCH UP

Match these Confederate governors with the state each served.

1. Joseph E. Brown   a) Alabama

2. Zebulon B. Vance   b) Arkansas

3. Francis W. Pickens   c) Florida

4. Harris Flanagin   d) Georgia

5. John J. Pettus   e) Louisiana

6. John Letcher   f) Mississippi

7. John Milton   g) North Carolina

8. Isham G. Harris   h) South Carolina

9. John G. Shorter   i) Tennessee

10. Thomas Overton Moore   j) Virginia

DIFFICULT

QUIZ 93
MULTIPLE CHOICE

1. Who was the only captain of the USS *Tuscumbia*?

   ❑ a. Samuel Howard   ❑ b. James W. Shirk
   ❑ c. Henry Walke   ❑ d. James P. Foster

2. Which Confederate general is credited with the invention of the landmine?

   ❑ a. Gabriel Rains   ❑ b. Nicholas Pierce
   ❑ c. John Echols   ❑ d. Alexander Campbell

3. Which Confederate general led the amphibious attack on Santa Rosa Island in 1861?

   ❑ a. James Chalmers
   ❑ b. James Patton Anderson
   ❑ c. Richard Heron Anderson
   ❑ d. John K. Jackson

4. Who led the Confederate land attack that retook Plymouth, North Carolina in 1864?

   ❑ a. Carter Stevenson   ❑ b. Daniel Ruggles
   ❑ c. William Ruffin Cox   ❑ d. Robert Hoke

5. Joseph E. Johnston died of pneumonia ten days after attending whose funeral?

   ❑ a. Ulysses S. Grant   ❑ b. William T. Sherman
   ❑ c. Robert E. Lee   ❑ d. Jefferson Davis

6. In the Union Army, the post of Signal Officer of the Army was equivalent to what standard Army rank?

   ❑ a. captain   ❑ b. major
   ❑ c. colonel   ❑ d. brigadier-general

7. What ship was packed with explosives and used as a floating bomb against Fort Fisher in Wilmington, North Carolina?

   ❑ a. USS *Mississippi*   ❑ b. USS *Louisiana*
   ❑ c. USS *Alabama*   ❑ d. USS *Missouri*

8. What was the last name of the Union nurse known variously as "Gentle Anne" or "Michigan Anne"?

   ❑ a. Burbank   ❑ b. Sprague
   ❑ c. Ruger   ❑ d. Etheridge

9. Which widow's house served as the headquarters for the Army of the Potomac during the battle of Gettysburg?

   ❑ a. Lydia Leister   ❑ b. Martha Anderson
   ❑ c. Elizabeth Haines   ❑ d. Catharine Tines

10. A Henry rifle carried how many shots when fully loaded?

   ❑ a. 12   ❑ b. 14
   ❑ c. 16   ❑ d. 18

ANAGRAMS

"Noble Josh Hit Wok"

(Answers on page 216)

QUIZ 94
TRUE OR FALSE

1. Dread Scott remained a slave his entire life.
   - ❑ True   ❑ False

2. "Joe Brown's Pikes" were used in battle by Confederate troops on two occasions.
   - ❑ True   ❑ False

3. Thomas Munford never received a commission as a general.
   - ❑ True   ❑ False

4. Paul Joseph Revere, grandson of the famous patriot Paul Revere, was mortally wounded at Antietam.
   - ❑ True   ❑ False

5. Confederate general Henry Hopkins Sibley was the father of Union general Henry Hastings Sibley.
   - ❑ True   ❑ False

6. The Massachusetts Institute of Technology was founded during the war.
   - ❑ True   ❑ False

7. The Confederacy minted no coins.
   - ❑ True   ❑ False

8. George Washington Custis Lee's childhood nickname was "Poop."
   - ❑ True   ❑ False

9. The North never lost an army commander in combat.
   - ❑ True   ❑ False

10. The writer of the song "Dixie" was a Yankee.
    - ❑ True   ❑ False

MULTIPLE CHOICE

1. What was the nickname of the 14th Brooklyn regiment?

   ❑ a. Fire Lions   ❑ b. Bobcats
   ❑ c. Red Legged Devils   ❑ d. Blue Giants

2. Which of these Union generals did NOT die of wounds received during Antietam?

   ❑ a. Israel B. Richardson   ❑ b. Isaac P. Rodman
   ❑ c. Joseph K.F. Mansfield   ❑ d. William J. Landram

3. Which of these Confederate generals did NOT die of wounds received during Antietam?

   ❑ a. Robert S. Garnett   ❑ b. Lawrence O. Branch
   ❑ c. George B. Anderson   ❑ d. William E. Starke

4. What type of photograph was most common during the war?

   ❑ a. daguerreotype   ❑ b. ambrotype
   ❑ c. ferrotype   ❑ d. carte de visite

DID YOU KNOW...

The original Constitution of the United States banned slavery; however, the state of Virginia refused to ratify it, and the slavery ban was removed.

5. Who invented the "wig-wag" system, used by signal corps throughout the war?

❑ a. Samuel Morse ❑ b. Albert Myer
❑ c. John Gibbon ❑ d. Joseph Gloskoski

6. Which regiment did Colonel Eppa Hunton lead during Ball's Bluff?

❑ a. 15th Alabama ❑ b. 8th Virginia
❑ c. 2nd Virginia ❑ d. 11th North Carolina

7. Who wrote *Company Aytch: Or a Side Show of the Big Show*?

❑ a. James D. McBride ❑ b. Samuel R. Watkins
❑ c. Henry W. Perkins ❑ d. Stephen Barker

8. Which of these engagements occurred last chronologically?

❑ a. Fort Stedman ❑ b. White Oak Road
❑ c. Lewis Farm ❑ d. Hatcher's Run

9. In which battle was Confederate general Stephen D. Ramseur mortally wounded?

❑ a. Monocacy ❑ b. Winchester
❑ c. Five Forks ❑ d. Cedar Creek

10. Which of the following was NOT a part of the battle of Chaffin's Farm?

❑ a. Fort Richards ❑ b. New Market Heights
❑ c. Laurel Hill ❑ d. Fort Gilmore

MATCH UP

Match these regiments with their nicknames.

1. 15th Wisconsin   a) Scandinavian Regiment

2. 2nd Massachusetts   b) Abbot Grays

3. 39th New York   c) Black Horse Cavalry

4. 79th New York   d) 1st US Hussars

5. 6th Pennsylvania Cavalry   e) Highlanders

6. 3rd New Jersey Cavalry   f) Rutledge's Cavalry

7. 13th Pennsylvania Reserves   g) Bucktails

8. 7th Louisiana   h) Garibaldi Guard

9. 4th Virginia Cavalry   i) Rush's Lancers

10. 4th South Carolina Cavalry   j) Pelicans

QUIZ 98
MULTIPLE CHOICE

1. Which Union gunboat was purposely destroyed by her commander in order to avoid capture during the 1863 battle of Galveston?

   ❑ a. USS *Clifton* ❑ b. USS *Owasco*
   ❑ c. USS *Sachem* ❑ d. USS *Westfield*

2. In which battle was Union general James Birdseye McPherson killed?

   ❑ a. Shiloh ❑ b. Corinth
   ❑ c. Atlanta ❑ d. Cold Harbor

3. Who was the only member of the Confederate Cabinet who voted against Robert E. Lee's second invasion of the north?

   ❑ a. Stephen R. Mallory ❑ b. Thomas H. Watts
   ❑ c. John H. Reagan ❑ d. Christopher G. Memminger

4. According to US Army regulations, how many chevrons did corporals wear on their sleeves?

   ❑ a. 0 ❑ b. 1
   ❑ c. 2 ❑ d. 3

5. Officers in the US Corps of Engineers wore what symbol on their cap badge?

   ❑ a. castle ❑ b. pick
   ❑ c. hammer ❑ d. bridge

6. Which Native American tribe was badly defeated at the 1863 battle of Whitestone Hill?

- a. Navajo
- b. Sioux
- c. Crow
- d. Arapaho

7. How many infantry regiments did the "Pennsylvania Reserves" contain?

- a. 6
- b. 10
- c. 13
- d. 18

8. How high was "High Bridge" which spanned the Appomattox and became the scene of a battle in 1865?

- a. 89ft
- b. 101ft
- c. 116ft
- d. 126ft

9. The original "Texas Brigade" contained two regiments of volunteers from Texas and one regiment of volunteers from which other state?

- a. Alabama
- b. Louisiana
- c. Georgia
- d. Mississippi

10. Artillerymen from which state served the famous siege mortar "Dictator" during the siege of Petersburg?

- a. New York
- b. New Jersey
- c. Rhode Island
- d. Connecticut

> *I never saw one of Jackson's couriers approach without expecting an order to assault the North Pole.*
>
> Richard S. Ewell

QUIZ 99
TRUE OR FALSE

1. Confederate Secretary of the Navy Stephen R. Mallory was born in Japan.
   - ❑ True   ❑ False

2. Fewer than 1,000 officers from the old regular US Army would serve the Union in the Civil War.
   - ❑ True   ❑ False

3. Only two infantry regiments from Maryland fought for the Confederacy.
   - ❑ True   ❑ False

4. Not a single Medal of Honor was awarded to any soldier for the fighting at Wilson's Creek.
   - ❑ True   ❑ False

5. Over half of the Union Army at the battle of Pea Ridge spoke German as their first language.
   - ❑ True   ❑ False

6. Philip Sheridan would eventually become only the third man in United States history to wear the four stars of a full general.
   - ❑ True   ❑ False

7. Dodge City, Kansas is named after Union general Grenville Dodge.
   - ❑ True   ❑ False

8. An annotated edition of *Mary Chesnut's Diary* won the 1982 Pulitzer Prize for History.
   - ❑ True   ❑ False

9. Moses Ezekiel, the famous sculptor and veteran of the battle of New Market, was also the first Jewish cadet admitted to the Virginia Military Institute.
   - ❑ True   ❑ False

10. All of John Brown's sons were killed during his famous raid.

❑ True ❑ False

THE DRAFT.

All other Methods of evading the Draft having failed, the above Disgraceful Scheme is to be attempted on the 10th.

SHORT ANSWER

1. Who was the United States Consul to Buenos Aires during the Civil War?

. . . .

© Simon Tofield

2. How many former Confederate generals fought in the Imperial Mexican Army during the Jurista Revolution?

   . . . .

3. Abraham Lincoln was a citizen of the United States and which older constitutional republic?

   . . . .

4. Which Union general had the platyfish, *Xiphophorus couchiana*, named in his honor?

   . . . .

5. In what town can you still see "Swamp Angel," the 200-pounder Parrott rifle used to shell Charleston?

   . . . .

6. Who was the Confederacy's only Postmaster General?

   . . . .

7. Which Union regiment at one point contained two future presidents?

   . . . .

8. The ironclad CSS *Atlanta* was converted from which blockade runner?

   . . . .

9. On what date were the Lincoln conspirators hanged?

   . . . .

10. Who killed General A.P. Hill?

   . . . .

QUIZ 101

MULTIPLE CHOICE, THE CONFEDERATE MEDICAL SERVICES

1. What cap symbol denoted membership of the Infirmary Corps?

   ❑ a. star   ❑ b. diamond
   ❑ c. snake   ❑ d. cross

2. What was Richmond's largest military hospital during the war?

   ❑ a. Tunnel Hill Hospital   ❑ b. Jackson Hospital
   ❑ c. Chimborazo Hospital   ❑ d. Seabrook Hospital

3. How many medical schools were operating in the South in 1861?

   ❑ a. 0   ❑ b. 4
   ❑ c. 12   ❑ d. 21

4. Who was the first acting surgeon-general of the Confederate Army?

   ❑ a. David C. DeLeon   ❑ b. Charles H. Smith
   ❑ c. Samuel Preston Moore   ❑ d. James Brown McCaw

5. What was the only medical school in the Confederacy to keep its doors open for most of the war?

   ❑ a. Atlanta Medical College
   ❑ b. University of Louisiana School of Medicine
   ❑ c. Medical College of Virginia
   ❑ d. Medical College of South Carolina

6. Who was the executive officer in charge of all of Petersburg's military hospitals during the nine-month siege of the city?

   ❑ a. Samuel Preston Moore   ❑ b. Charles H. Smith
   ❑ c. John Claiborne   ❑ d. Pierre Paul Noel d'Alvigny

7. Who was the medical director of the Army of Northern Virginia for all of its major campaigns?

   ❑ a. Bedford Brown   ❑ b. Lafayette Guild
   ❑ c. James Brown McCaw   ❑ d. Edward Samuel Guillard

8. Confederate regulations allowed for how many ambulances per regiment in the field?

   ❑ a. 0   ❑ b. 2
   ❑ c. 4   ❑ d. 6

9. Which of these was NOT a Confederate Army hospital in South Carolina?

   ❑ a. Ladies' General No. 3   ❑ b. First Louisiana
   ❑ c. Soldier's Relief   ❑ d. Empire

10. Who saved the Atlanta Medical College from Sherman's torches?

   ❑ a. Dr William A. Carrigan
   ❑ b. Surgeon H.V. Miller
   ❑ c. Dr Pierre Paul Noel d'Alvigny
   ❑ d. Medical Director Hunter Holmes McGuire

From this time forward I ask no quarter and give none.

William "Bloody Bill" Anderson

MATCH UP

Match these commanders with their battlefield victories.

1. Joseph Reynolds a) Fort Blakely

2. Harvey Brown b) Hatchie's Bridge

3. Edward O.C. Ord c) Baxter Springs

4. James G. Blunt d) Santa Rosa Island

5. Benjamin H. Prentiss e) Mark's Mill

6. James F. Fagan f) Helena

7. Edward Canby g) Second Sabine Pass

8. William T. Sherman h) Cheat Mountain

9. Richard W. Dowling i) Ezra Church

10. William C. Quantrill j) Old Fort Wayne

QUIZ 103
FAMOUS FACES

Name these major Civil War figures.

DIFFICULT

1.

2.

3.

4.

5.

6.

ANSWERS

QUIZ 68 – MULTIPLE CHOICE
1)a 2)c 3)b 4)b 5)c 6)c 7)a 8)c 9)c 10)d

QUIZ 69 – TRUE OR FALSE
1) False
2) True
3) False. He suffered one casualty
4) False. It was repealed in 1864
5) True
6) True
7) True
8) False. Twenty were commissioned
9) True
10) True

QUIZ 70 – SHORT ANSWER
1) A surgeon
2) The District of Columbia
3) Spotsylvania Courthouse and Nashville, both are correct
4) Corps of Topographical Engineers
5) William Farquhar Barry
6) Aeronautic Department and Balloon Corps
7) Edwin H. Stoughton
8) 11th Florida Volunteers
9) Female sutlers who accompanied Zouave regiments
10) Albert James Myer

QUIZ 71 – MULTIPLE CHOICE, RAPHAEL SEMMES AND THE CSS *ALABAMA*
1)d 2)a 3)c 4)d 5)b 6)c 7)c 8)b 9)b 10)b

QUIZ 72 – MATCH UP
1)a 2)e 3)j 4)b 5)h 6)c 7)i 8)g 9)d 10)f

QUIZ 73 – MULTIPLE CHOICE
1)b 2)a 3)a 4)c 5)d 6)c 7)d 8)c 9)a 10)d

QUIZ 74 – TRUE OR FALSE
1) False
2) True
3) False. It was run by civilians throughout the war

4) True

5) True. Grant declined

6) False. Slavery was also still legal in Brazil and Cuba

7) True. The only President ever to have done so

8) False

9) True. There are over 400

10) True. During the battle of Carricitos Ranch

QUIZ 75 – SHORT ANSWER

1) Yes. Though it was more commonly called "All Fools Day"

2) The Petersburg Express

3) Gustavus Vasa Fox

4) John Basil Turchin

5) General Richard Taylor

6) Camp Sumter

7) Martin Van Buren and John Tyler

8) Dr J.B. Peters

9) Vice admiral

10) Philip Kearney

QUIZ 76 – MULTIPLE CHOICE

1)c 2)d 3)a 4)b 5)b 6)c 7)c 8)a 9)b 10)c

QUIZ 77 – MATCH UP

1)d 2)j 3)i 4)g 5)c 6)a 7)f 8)e 9)h 10)b

QUIZ 78 – MULTIPLE CHOICE

1)c 2)a 3)c 4)b 5)d 6)d 7)c 8)d 9)a 10)b

QUIZ 79 – TRUE OR FALSE

1) True

2) False. Some are thought to have served, but none were ever captured

3) False. They were used by France during its invasion of Italy in 1859

4) True

5) True. It is closer to 55 percent

6) True

7) True

8) True

9) False. The Navy Medal of Honor was instituted in 1861, the year before the Army version

10) True

QUIZ 80 – SHORT ANSWER

1) Dysentery
2) Union. Among many things, he served as chief engineer for Sherman
3) John Taylor Wood, grandson of former President Zachary Taylor
4) Benito Juárez
5) William H. Lytle
6) CSS *Patrick Henry*
7) Mercury
8) "J" because it looked too much like "I"
9) Lew Wallace
10) Gerald Ford

QUIZ 81 – MULTIPLE CHOICE, JOSHUA CHAMBERLAIN AND THE 20TH MAINE

1)c 2)a 3)d 4)c 5)b 6)b 7)b 8)a 9)d 10)a

QUIZ 82 – MATCH UP

1)a 2)h 3)c 4)g 5)j 6)f 7)e 8)b 9)i 10)d

QUIZ 83 – MULTIPLE CHOICE

1)a 2)a 3)b 4)b 5)c 6)d 7)b 8)c 9)d 10)c

QUIZ 84 – TRUE OR FALSE

1) False. Nearly 20,000 slaves were freed in Union-held Confederate territory
2) True
3) False. They carried lances until May 1863
4) False. It was first used during the Seven Days Battles
5) True. In 1833
6) False
7) True. He was a co-founder
8) True
9) True
10) True

QUIZ 85 – SHORT ANSWER

1) Knights of the Golden Circle
2) Brigadier-General Seth Williams
3) Gibraltar
4) "Useless, useless"
5) None
6) Colonel George H. Sharpe
7) Stand Watie

8) British Enfield

9) Members of the Signal Corps

10) Spencer rifle

QUIZ 86 – MULTIPLE CHOICE
1)d 2)a 3)b 4)c 5)a 6)a 7)c 8)d 9)c 10)a

QUIZ 87 – MATCH UP
1)g 2)b 3)h 4)a 5)f 6)j 7)c 8)d 9)i 10)e

QUIZ 88 – MULTIPLE CHOICE
1)d 2)c 3)d 4)a 5)b 6)b 7)c 8)b 9)a 10)d

QUIZ 89 – TRUE OR FALSE
1) True

2) True. It was closer to $4 million

3) True. A few days before the surrender at Appomattox Courthouse

4) False

5) True. Provided they wrote "soldier's letter" on the envelope

6) True. Provided the bearer complies with all Federal, State, and local laws

7) True

8) False. The Union forces retreated

9) True

10) False. She died in 1962

QUIZ 90 – SHORT ANSWER
1) Senator Benjamin Wade

2) Daniel Harvey Hill

3) Prussia

4) Simon Bolivar Buckner, who died in 1914

5) USS *Powhatan*

6) John Mercer Brooke

7) Dr Mary Edwards Walker

8) North Carolina

9) One. CSS *Stonewall*

10) Union general Jefferson C. Davis

QUIZ 91 – MULTIPLE CHOICE, THOMAS FRANCIS MEAGHER AND THE IRISH BRIGADE
1)d 2)b 3)a 4)b 5)d 6)c 7)d 8)c 9)c 10)b

QUIZ 92 – MATCH UP
1)d 2)g 3)h 4)b 5)f 6)j 7)c 8)i 9)a 10)e

QUIZ 93 – MULTIPLE CHOICE
1)b 2)a 3)c 4)d 5)b 6)c 7)b 8)d 9)a 10)c

QUIZ 94 – TRUE OR FALSE
1) False. He spent his last year as a free man
2) False. They were never used in battle
3) False. Although his commission was never confirmed
4) False. He recovered from the wound at Antietam and was mortally wounded at Gettysburg
5) False
6) True
7) False. A limited number of dollar and half-dollar coins were minted in New Orleans before the fall of the city
8) False. It was "Boo"
9) False. General James Birdseye McPherson died leading his army in the battle of Atlanta
10) True. Composer Daniel Emmet was born in Ohio

QUIZ 95 – SHORT ANSWER
1) Youth gangs in Richmond
2) Hugh Judson Kilpatrick
3) USS *Cairo*
4) Robert S. Garnett
5) Post-Traumatic Stress Disorder (or "shell shock")
6) An acorn
7) Colonel Marcus Spiegel, 67th Ohio
8) John Burns
9) South. The nickname was used for Southern peace-seekers
10) Oliver Otis Howard

QUIZ 96 – MULTIPLE CHOICE
1)c 2)d 3)a 4)c 5)b 6)b 7)b 8)b 9)d 10)a

QUIZ 97 – MATCH UP
1)a 2)b 3)h 4)e 5)i 6)d 7)g 8)j 9)c 10)f

QUIZ 98 – MULTIPLE CHOICE
1)d 2)c 3)c 4)c 5)a 6)b 7)c 8)d 9)c 10)d

QUIZ 99 – TRUE OR FALSE
1) False. He was born in Trinidad
2) True
3) True

4) False. Five were awarded

5) False. But it was close

6) False. He was the fourth. Washington, Grant, and Sherman all preceded him

7) True

8) True

9) True

10) False. One survived

QUIZ 100 – SHORT ANSWER

1) Hinton R. Helper, author of *The Impending Crisis*

2) Four. Mosby Parsons, Sterling Price, John Magruder, and Joseph Shelby

3) San Marino, which extended citizenship to him in 1861

4) Darius Couch

5) Trenton, New Jersey

6) John H. Reagan

7) 23rd Ohio, which contained Rutherford B. Hayes and William McKinley

8) *Fingal*

9) July 7, 1865

10) Corporal John Mauck (though Private Daniel Wolford also claimed credit)

QUIZ 101 – MULTIPLE CHOICE, THE CONFEDERATE MEDICAL SERVICES

1)b 2)c 3)d 4)a 5)c 6)b 7)b 8)c 9)d 10)c

QUIZ 102 – MATCH UP

1)h 2)d 3)b 4)j 5)f 6)e 7)a 8)i 9)g 10)c

QUIZ 103 – FAMOUS FACES

1) William F. Barry, Union artillery general

2) Stephen R. Mallory, Confederate Secretary of the Navy

3) Simon B. Buckner, Confederate general

4) Edwin V. Sumner, Union general

5) Edward Canby, Union general

6) Darius Couch, Union general

IMPOSSIBLE
QUESTIONS

FOUR-STAR
GENERAL
KNOWLEDGE

MULTIPLE CHOICE

1. According to the 1861 "Regulations for the Army of the Confederate States" the rank of "Cadet" was just below which other rank?

   ❑ a. second lieutenant   ❑ b. sergeant-major
   ❑ c. corporal   ❑ d. private

2. Which Confederate general was sometimes known as "The Bengal Tiger"?

   ❑ a. Hiram Bronson Granbury
   ❑ b. James Cantey
   ❑ c. David Emanuel Twiggs
   ❑ d. Chatham Wheat

3. What was the first vessel built specifically to run the Union blockade?

   ❑ a. *Ceres*   ❑ b. *Margaret and Jesse*
   ❑ c. *Banshee* ❑ d. *Cornubia*

4. What was the first song published in the Confederacy?

   ❑ a. *Bonnie Blue Flag*   ❑ b. *Dixie*
   ❑ c. *God Save the South* ❑ d. *My Old Kentucky Home*

5. Which of these blockade runners did John Wilkinson never command?

   ❑ a. *Dare*   ❑ b. *Robert E. Lee*
   ❑ c. *Chickamauga* ❑ d. *Chameleon*

6. Which cavalry regiment captured Jefferson Davis?

   ❏ a. 1st Michigan Cavalry   ❏ b. 2nd Michigan Cavalry
   ❏ c. 3rd Michigan Cavalry   ❏ d. 4th Michigan Cavalry

7. Who led the Confederate forces in the 1865 battle of
   Palmetto Ranch?

   ❏ a. Colonel John S. Ford
   ❏ b. Colonel Theodore H. Barrett
   ❏ c. Colonel Robert B. Jones
   ❏ d. Captain George Roberson

8. What was the minimum age of volunteers for the 37th Iowa
   "Greybeard" regiment?

   ❏ a. 30   ❏ b. 45
   ❏ c. 55   ❏ d. 65

9. Union general Alexander Asboth was a native of what country?

   ❏ a. Russia   ❏ b. Romania
   ❏ c. Hungary   ❏ d. Canada

10. Who presided over the Convention of Seceded States in
    Montgomery, Alabama which began on February 4, 1861?

   ❏ a. John Slidell   ❏ b. Howell Cobb
   ❏ c. Judah Benjamin   ❏ d. Alexander Stephens

IMPOSSIBLE

*These men were our enemies a moment ago; they are our
prisoners now. Take care of them.*

Albert Sidney Johnston to his doctor before he bled to death

QUIZ 105
MULTIPLE CHOICE

1. Which Pope urged his bishops to preach peace in the United States in 1863?

   ☐ a. Pius VI ☐ b. Julius III
   ☐ c. Pius IX ☐ d. Benedict VIII

2. During the war, how many different official "armies" did the North field?

   ☐ a. 12 ☐ b. 16
   ☐ c. 20 ☐ d. 23

3. Who was the last slave returned under the Fugitive Slave Law?

   ☐ a. Susie Stanes ☐ b. Elizabeth Reams
   ☐ c. Eliza Jones ☐ d. Lucy Bagby

4. What was the most-purchased newspaper in America in 1860?

   ☐ a. *New York Herald* ☐ b. *New York Times*
   ☐ c. *New York Tribune* ☐ d. *Harper's Weekly Journal of Civilization*

5. After Andersonville, which prisoner-of-war camp experienced the most deaths amongst its prisoners?

   ☐ a. Point Lookout ☐ b. Salisbury
   ☐ c. Camp Douglas ☐ d. Elmira

6. Who wrote the words to the song "Stonewall Jackson's Way"?

   ❏ a. John P. Darbey   ❏ b. John W. Palmer
   ❏ c. Gerard S. Walker   ❏ d. Henry A. Wise

7. Which former Union general became the first president of the National Rifle Association?

   ❏ a. Joseph Hooker   ❏ b. Ambrose Burnside
   ❏ c. John M. Schofield   ❏ d. Ulysses S. Grant

8. In the Union Army, which of these positions was the highest paid?

   ❏ a. bugler   ❏ b. wagoner
   ❏ c. infantry private   ❏ d. artillery artificer

9. Which cemetery holds the bodies of the most Civil War soldiers killed during the war?

   ❏ a. Arlington National Cemetery
   ❏ b. Hollywood Cemetery
   ❏ c. Oakwood Cemetery
   ❏ d. Blandford Church Cemetery

10. Which of the following regiments was NOT part of the Corcoran Legion?

   ❏ a. 155th New York   ❏ b. 162nd New York
   ❏ c. 170th New York   ❏ d. 182nd New York

ANAGRAMS

"Licenses Work"

(Answers on page 216)

QUIZ 106
MULTIPLE CHOICE

1. Who was the first Confederate States Commissioner for Indian Affairs?

   ❑ a. Isaac M. St John   ❑ b. David Hubbard
   ❑ c. Alexander R. Lawton   ❑ d. Richard Morton

2. Which chief led the Cheyenne and Arapaho who were betrayed and attacked at the Sand Creek Massacre in 1864?

   ❑ a. Two-hatchet   ❑ b. Black Horse
   ❑ c. Black Kettle   ❑ d. Roman Nose

3. Who served as the US Army representative to the second inauguration of Abraham Lincoln?

   ❑ a. William Rosencranz   ❑ b. Ambrose Burnside
   ❑ c. Winfield Hancock   ❑ d. Joseph Hooker

4. What date was the "Black Thursday of the Confederacy"?

   ❑ a. April 6, 1865   ❑ b. April 17, 1865
   ❑ c. April 28, 1865   ❑ d. May 5, 1865

5. What was the name of the settlement provided by Emperor Maximilian to fleeing Confederates?

   ❑ a. Delia   ❑ b. Carlota
   ❑ c. Refuge   ❑ d. Freedom

6. During the war, Henry Shelton Sanford served as the US Minister to which European country?

❑ a. Holland ❑ b. Poland
❑ c. Italy ❑ d. Belgium

7. Who was the top-ranking naval surgeon of the Confederacy?

   ❑ a. Andrew J. Foard ❑ b. William A. W. Spotswood
   ❑ c. Samuel H. Stout ❑ d. Caleb C. Herbert

8. Which noted landscape architect designed the "Soldiers' National Cemetery" at Gettysburg?

   ❑ a. Capability Brown ❑ b. William Saunders
   ❑ c. Fletcher Steele ❑ d. Frederick Law Olmstead

9. General Grant's adjutant, Ely Parker, who wrote out the Appomattox surrender terms, was a Native American of which tribe?

   ❑ a. Cherokee ❑ b. Shawnee
   ❑ c. Seneca ❑ d. Fox

10. Discounting brevets, which of these men was NOT a general officer during the war?

    ❑ a. Egbert Ludovickus Viele
    ❑ b. Victor Vifquain
    ❑ c. John Bordenave Villepigue
    ❑ d. Ferdinand Van Derveer

I cannot guess Hood's movements as I could those of Johnston, who was a sensible man and only did sensible things.

William T. Sherman

QUIZ 107
MULTIPLE CHOICE

1. In which of these battles was Union general James B. Ricketts NOT wounded?

   ❏ a. First Manassas
   ❏ b. Antietam
   ❏ c. Gettysburg
   ❏ d. Cedar Creek

2. What was the first United States vessel ever captured by Confederate forces?

   ❏ a. *Fanny*
   ❏ b. *Carolyn*
   ❏ c. *Sarah Sea*
   ❏ d. *Emily*

3. Which of these Union major-generals lived the longest?

   ❏ a. Franz Sigel
   ❏ b. Peter Joseph Osterhaus
   ❏ c. Samuel Ryan Curtis
   ❏ d. Alexander Schimmelfennig

4. Who led the Confederates that held off the attack on Staunton River Bridge in 1864?

   ❏ a. Benjamin Fairnholt
   ❏ b. Arthur Bagby
   ❏ c. John Shorter
   ❏ d. William Bate

5. The 1865 battle of Natural Bridge was fought over which Florida river?

   ❏ a. St Marys
   ❏ b. Trout
   ❏ c. Indian
   ❏ d. St Marks

6. Which of these is NOT another name for the 1865 battle of Averasborough?

   ❑ a. Harnett Farm   ❑ b. Taylor's Hole Creek
   ❑ c. Smiths Ferry   ❑ d. Black River

7. Which of these battles occurred last chronologically?

   ❑ a. Big Mound   ❑ b. Dead Buffalo Lake
   ❑ c. Stony Lake   ❑ d. Killdeer Mountain

8. According to the Civil War Sites Advisory Commission, established by Congress in 1990, how many battlefield sites were identified as "class A" (battles having a decisive influence on a campaign and a direct impact on the course of the war)?

   ❑ a. 12   ❑ b. 28
   ❑ c. 45   ❑ d. 62

9. "Opdycke's Tigers" was the nickname of which Ohio regiment?

   ❑ a. 66th   ❑ b. 86th
   ❑ c. 99th   ❑ d. 125th

10. Which of these universities did Confederate general John Sappington Marmaduke NOT attend?

   ❑ a. West Point   ❑ b. Harvard
   ❑ c. Princeton   ❑ d. Yale

Enough lives have been extinguished. We must extinguish our resentments if we expect harmony and union.

Abraham Lincoln

QUIZ 108
MULTIPLE CHOICE

1. Who was the highest-ranking member of the "Fighting McCooks"?

   ❑ a. Robert Latimer McCook
   ❑ b. Henry Christopher McCook
   ❑ c. John James McCook
   ❑ d. Alexander McDowell McCook

© Simon Tofield

IMPOSSIBLE

2. During the Civil War, what was the only Native American tribe to have a written form of their language?

   ❑ a. Choctaw ❑ b. Creek
   ❑ c. Seminole ❑ d. Cherokee

3. Who was the Confederate Agent in Bermuda?

   ❑ a. Edward N. Covey ❑ b. Norman Walker
   ❑ c. James B. Read ❑ d. Joseph Jones

4. Which Union general went on to write *Corporal S. Klegg and His "Pard"*?

   ❑ a. William F. Hinman ❑ b. Henry Bohlen
   ❑ c. Albion P. Howe ❑ d. David Hunter

5. How many barrels did the Billinghurst Requa Battery have?

   ❑ a. 5 ❑ b. 10
   ❑ c. 15 ❑ d. 25

6. In what year was the USS *Cairo* raised from the Yazoo River?

   ❑ a. 1954 ❑ b. 1964
   ❑ c. 1974 ❑ d. 1984

7. What was the original name of the blockade runner rechristened *Robert E. Lee*?

   ❑ a. *Giraffe* ❑ b. *Annie*
   ❑ c. *Elephant* ❑ d. *Ella*

8. "Cobb's Legion" was raised in which state?

   ❑ a. Georgia ❑ b. South Carolina
   ❑ c. North Carolina ❑ d. Virginia

9. Which vessel can claim the honor of being the war's first aircraft carrier, having launched an observation balloon in 1861?

☐ a. USS *George Washington Parke Custis*
☐ b. USS *Eagle*
☐ c. USS *Fanny*
☐ d. USS *May Flower*

10. Who led the 16th South Carolina Volunteers at the battle of Franklin?

☐ a. James McCullough ☐ b. Edward Farnsworth
☐ c. John Stewart Walker ☐ d. Simon Timpson

DID YOU KNOW...

As Sherman's men moved through Atlanta setting torches to the buildings, they encountered Atlanta's last doctor, the aged Pierre Paul Noel d'Alvigny, standing on the steps of the Atlanta Medical College. The venerable doctor shouted to the men that they couldn't burn the College, as he still had patients inside. After seeing that there were indeed sick men in the beds, the soldiers gave d'Alvigny one day to move the sick out before they returned with their torches. The next day, Sherman's army marched out of the city before the soldiers could carry out their threat. The College was safe, and Dr d'Alvigny could concentrate on helping the members of his staff recover from their whiskey-induced "sickness."

QUIZ 109
FAMOUS FACES

Name these major Civil War figures.

1.

2.

3.

4.

5.

6.

 214

My troops may fail to take a position, but are never driven from one.

Thomas J. "Stonewall" Jackson

7.   8.   9.

10.   11.   12.